W9-BAZ-949

2

THE IMPORTANCE OF

Jackie Robinson

by
Arthur Diamond

Lucent Books, P.O. Box 289011, San Diego, CA 92198-9011

Acknowledgment

The author wishes to thank Bonnie Szumski
for her hand in the creation of this book.

Dedication

To Benjamin and Jessica

These and other titles are included in The Importance Of
biography series:

Benjamin Franklin	Galileo Galilei
Chief Joseph	Richard M. Nixon
Christopher Columbus	Jackie Robinson
Marie Curie	H.G. Wells

Library of Congress Cataloging-in-Publication Data

Diamond, Arthur, 1957–
    Jackie Robinson / by Arthur Diamond
    p. cm.—(The Importance of)
    Includes bibliographical references and index.
Summary: Examines the life of the first black man to play in
major league baseball.
    ISBN 1-56006-029-8
    1. Robinson, Jackie, 1919–1972—Juvenile literature.
2. Baseball players—United States—Biography—Juvenile literature. [1. Robinson, Jackie, 1919–1972. 2. Baseball players.
3. Afro-Americans—Biography.]
I. Title. II. Series.
GV865.R6D53   1992
796.375'092—dc20   92-19871
[B]   CIP
                                                                   AC

Copyright 1992 by Lucent Books, Inc., P.O. Box 289011, San
Diego, California, 92198-9011

Contents

Foreword

THE IMPORTANCE OF biography series deals with individuals who have made a unique contribution to history. The editors of the series have deliberately chosen to cast a wide net and include people from all fields of endeavor. Individuals from politics, music, art, literature, philosophy, science, sports, and religion are all represented. In addition, the editors did not restrict the series to individuals whose accomplishments have helped change the course of history. Of necessity, this criterion would have eliminated many whose contribution was great, though limited. Charles Darwin, for example, was responsible for radically altering the scientific view of the natural history of the world. His achievements continue to impact the study of science today. Others, such as Chief Joseph of the Nez Percé, played a pivotal role in the history of their own people. While Joseph's influence does not extend much beyond the Nez Percé, his nonviolent resistance to white expansion and his continuing role in protecting his tribe and his homeland remain an inspiration to all.

These biographies are more than factual chronicles. Each volume attempts to emphasize an individual's contributions both in his or her own time and for posterity. For example, the voyages of Christopher Columbus opened the way to European colonization of the New World. Unquestionably, his encounter with the New World brought monumental changes to both Europe and the Americas in his day. Today, however, the broader impact of Columbus's voyages is being critically scrutinized. *Christopher Columbus,* as well as every biography in The Importance Of series, includes and evaluates the most recent scholarship available on each subject.

Each author includes a wide variety of primary and secondary source quotations to document and substantiate his or her work. All quotes are footnoted to show readers exactly how and where biographers derive their information, as well as provide stepping stones to further research. These quotations enliven the text by giving readers eyewitness views of the life and times of each individual covered in The Importance Of series.

Finally, each volume is enhanced by photographs, bibliographies, chronologies, and comprehensive indexes. For both the casual reader and the student engaged in research, The Importance Of biographies will be a fascinating adventure into the lives of people who have helped shape humanity's past, present, and will continue to shape its future.

Important Dates in the Life of Jackie Robinson

Jack Roosevelt Robinson born on January 31 to Jerry and Mallie Robinson of Cairo, Georgia.	**1919** **1920**	Mallie Robinson and her five children move to Pasadena, California.
On July 6, at Fort Hood, Texas, Robinson refuses army bus driver's demand to move to back of bus.	**1944** **1945**	Historic meeting with Branch Rickey in New York, on August 28. Press conference on October 23 announces the signing of Jackie Robinson to the Brooklyn Dodgers.
Marries his college sweetheart, Rachel Isum, in February. Plays in first game for Montreal Royals on April 18.	**1946**	
	1947	Plays in first game for Brooklyn Dodgers on April 15. Voted Rookie of the Year.
First and only World Series win for Robinson with the Dodgers (over Yankees), on October 4.	**1949** **1955**	Gives speech on July 18 to the House Committee on Un-American Activities criticizing Paul Robeson. Voted National League's Most Valuable Player.
Officially announces retirement from baseball in January.	**1957** **1960**	Campaigns for Richard Nixon for president.
Inducted into National Baseball Hall of Fame in July.	**1962** **1968**	Campaigns for Hubert Humphrey for president.
Son Jackie Jr., dies in automobile accident on June 17.	**1971** **1972**	Jackie Robinson dies at age 53 in Stamford, Connecticut on October 24.

Something to Remember

The year 1946 was a somber one in the history of the United States. There had been victory overseas in World War II, but at home the war against equal rights for blacks continued. The National Association for the Advancement of Colored People (NAACP) reported that some returning black veterans had been victims of "blowtorch killing and eye-gouging." At least nine blacks were lynched in the United States. Newspaper photographs from around the country showed the corpses of innocent blacks swinging from trees, hung by the neck.

April 18 of that year was opening day for the International League, a minor league made up of clubs, or farm teams, of professional baseball's major league teams. The Montreal Royals, the top farm team of the Brooklyn Dodgers, began their season that day in New Jersey, against the Jersey City Giants.

After the first batter for the Royals grounded out, the second batter emerged from the dugout and strode to home plate. As his name was announced over the stadium loudspeakers, the fans—some fifty thousand of them—acknowledged his presence with polite applause. Despite the reserved welcome, every pair of eyes in the stadium was on him. This second batter for the Royals was Jackie Robinson, and he was the first black man to play in major league baseball.

Every Royals player dreamed of being called up by the Dodgers to play in the big leagues, and on this day Robinson knew that his chances for going to the Dodgers were fairly strong. Dodgers manager Branch Rickey had signed Robinson to a contract with the Dodgers a few months before, but first Robinson had to spend a crucial season proving himself worthy before he could be promoted to the major leagues.

Standing at home plate, awaiting the pitcher's throw, Jackie Robinson became a symbol for the emerging demand for black equality in the United States. Blacks were demanding to be integrated into American society, and many factors contributed to

Jackie Robinson warms up for batting practice at his first spring training camp in 1946.

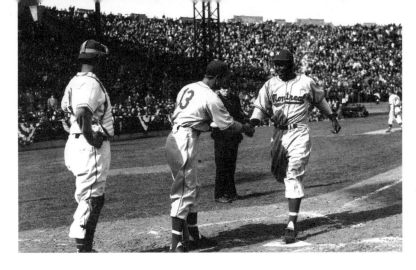

Jackie Robinson gets a handshake from teammate George Shuba after hitting a three-run homer in his first professional game.

integration's slow success. These factors included blacks' heroics in World War II, the efforts of the NAACP, the courageous legislation in favor of civil rights put forth by President Franklin D. Roosevelt, and the countless brave and lonely stands taken by many individuals in the face of racism. Now a black man stood at home plate, wearing the same uniform as any white baseball player, holding his bat the same way, and with the opportunity to prove to the world that he was just as good as anybody else.

Robinson nervously awaited the first pitch. Later he would recall that his palms seemed "too moist to hold the bat." He did not move as the first pitch sped by him and out of the strike zone. He took a deep breath and awaited the next pitch. He did not swing at that one either, nor at the following three pitches, and the count was full at three balls and two strikes. On the sixth pitch Robinson swung and connected—but the batted ball didn't leave the infield. The shortstop on the Giants caught the weak grounder and threw Robinson out at first base.

His next time up at bat would be different. In the third inning, Robinson returned to the plate. There were already two men on base, and everyone in the ballpark expected Robinson to bunt. By doing so, he would advance the runners while sacrificing himself. But Robinson had other ideas.

The pitcher threw a fast ball high into the strike zone—difficult for anyone to bunt—and Robinson leaned into the pitch and swung mightily. The audience gasped as bat met ball, and fans jumped to their feet to watch the ball sail like a rocket into left field and disappear beyond the fence. It was a home run, scoring three runs. Robinson jogged around the bases, grinning. The third base coach for the Royals, a white man from Mississippi named Clay Hopper, patted Robinson on the back. The next batter up, George Shuba, a white man from Youngstown, Ohio, reached out and shook Robinson's hand.

The photograph that appeared the next morning in the New Jersey papers was different from the usual sports pictures. While photographs of lynchings lingered in the minds of Americans, there was a new image of black America to focus on, study, and remember. As George Shuba recalled, "It was the first picture of a black player being congratulated by a white player for a home run."[1]

Chapter

1 Early Life

Jack Roosevelt Robinson was born on January 31, 1919, the youngest child of Jerry and Mallie Robinson of rural Cairo, Georgia. Six months after Jackie's birth his father abandoned the family. Distraught and desperate, Mallie Robinson moved Jackie, his three brothers, Frank, Edgar, and Mack, and his sister Willa Mae, to Pasadena, California.

In California during the 1920s there were laws against racial intermarriage and equality in schools, and laws prohibited blacks from testifying in court. Even so, blacks still found better treatment in the western states than in other parts of the country. As black scholar W. Sherman Savage asserts, "For most black people, the

As recently as 1962, this sign segregated blacks from whites in a Mississippi train station. The Robinsons, like many blacks, tried to escape southern racism by moving west.

West was not the Promised Land. But neither were its restrictions as severe as those which they had known in the South and the East. On balance, the West has given blacks an opportunity to make a better life for themselves."[2]

Mallie Robinson had come to California to make a better life for her family. In Pasadena they stayed with Mallie's brother Burton until they bought a house of their own on Pepper Street, in an all-white, lower middle-class neighborhood. Mallie worked night and day as a domestic servant for white families so she could afford to raise her children on Pepper Street. But she was not prepared for the conditions blacks faced in Pasadena, where neighborhoods were either all white or all black. Most blacks in Pasadena lived in crowded apartments in run-down neighborhoods, while most whites lived on clean, tree-lined streets. When the Robinsons challenged this status quo by moving to Pepper Street, neighbors made it clear that they wanted the black family to leave and harassed the Robinsons.

One day a neighbor summoned the police to protest the noise of Edgar Robinson's skates on the sidewalk; Mallie Robinson was kindly informed by the police officer that the woman across the street was "afraid of colored people." Neighbors banded together against the Robinsons, and a petition was handed from house to house and signed by many. The petition was designed to scare the Robinsons away—the neighbors had no legal power to make the family move. When the Robinsons ignored the document, they were approached by representatives of the community, who wanted to buy their house. But Mallie Robinson declared that she had no intention of selling. She was staying right where she was.

Bigotry

For the Robinsons and other blacks, living in Pasadena meant a constant encounter with the forces of bigotry. Mack Robinson, one of Jackie's older brothers, recalled the difficulty of living in Pasadena: "What my mother didn't know when she brought us here, what none of us knew, was that Pasadena was as prejudiced as any town in the South. They let us in all right, but they wouldn't let us live."[3]

Young Jackie grew up with a reservoir of pride and a razor-sharp temper. He had his share of experiences with bigotry and he always tried to fight back. According to Jackie's sister Willa Mae, "We always worried about him because he was so quick to anger if somebody said something that was insulting. I don't think Jack ever looked for a fight, but I don't think he ever walked away from one, neither."[4]

Mallie Robinson encouraged Jackie's attitude. She reminded her children that they must fight back when it was necessary. The granddaughter of a slave, she kept her composure when she felt insulted or threatened—especially because of the color of her skin—but she never allowed herself to be intimidated. She always made it clear that she was afraid of no one.

A loving boy, Jackie desired to stay close to home, to be near his mother, and years later he would recall the bond he had with her: "I remember, even as a small boy, having a lot of pride in my mother. I thought she must have some kind of magic to be able to do all the things she did, to work so hard and never complain and to make us feel happy. . . . My pride in my mother was tempered with a sense of sadness that she had to bear most of our

Jackie Robinson (far right) poses with classmates and teachers for a junior high school picture. The future Hall of Famer was already an outstanding athlete by this time.

burdens. At a very early age I began to want to relieve her in any small way I could. I was happy whenever I had money to give her."[5]

An Aptitude for Sports

From an early age, Jackie showed an aptitude for sports of all kinds, and his siblings, who were also excellent athletes, encouraged him. Each helped the others improve. Edgar, the oldest, was a great roller skater and loved to play softball. Frank, next to the oldest, was a sprinter. His favorite event was the hundred-yard dash, and his time was always close to the world record. Willa Mae was on every team she could join. Besides playing on school soccer, basketball, and track teams, she was a fine sprinter, too. As Jackie later recalled, "We had our family squabbles and spats, but we were a well-knit unit."[6]

Jackie's athletic abilities did not go unnoticed by his grammar school friends: he was frequently offered dimes or cookies to agree to play on someone's team! He soon found that he was extremely adept at any sport he tried. Tom Mallory, who was Robinson's football coach at Pasadena

Junior College (now Pasadena City College), remembered Jackie's innate ability:

> He excelled at every sport, not only the team sports, the individual sports, too. He was a great ping-pong player. He was a wonderful handball player. He played badminton. He was just so damn quick in every sport that he could play every game with ease. He was a great dribbler in basketball and could fake guys right out of the play. I remember when I had him in football, and we were playing Compton Junior College and he was coming down the field toward our side and there were four Compton guys converging on him. He rolled one way, faked another, and the four Compton guys crashed out of bounds onto our bench as Jackie ran in untouched for a score.[7]

A Young Rebel

As Jackie entered adolescence, the constant bigotry he faced made him rebellious. He began getting into trouble with a spirited group of boys called the Pepper

Street Gang. The gang was made up of black, Mexican, and Japanese boys from the neighborhood. They were not violent, but they ended up in trouble on a regular basis for throwing dirt at cars, stealing golf balls from the local golf course, and stealing fruit from neighborhood stands.

Two black men in the community saw what was happening and approached Jackie. One of them was Carl Anderson, who worked as a mechanic at a local garage. Years later Robinson remembered his first meeting with Anderson:

> After he had watched us for a while, he took me aside and talked to me about the gang. He didn't scold me, and he approached the subject from a point of view I couldn't ignore. He made me see that if I continued with the gang it would hurt my mother as well as myself. He told me I ought to admit to myself that I didn't belong in a gang, that I was simply following the crowd because I was afraid of being thought different, of being "chicken." He said it didn't take guts to follow the crowd, that courage and intelligence lay in being willing to be different. I was too ashamed to tell Carl how right he was, but what he said got to me.[8]

The other man who steered Robinson away from crime was the Reverend Karl Downs, pastor of the Robinsons' church. A young man new to Pasadena, Downs was enthusiastic about drawing the children of the community to the church. He instituted new programs and encouraged youngsters to plan dances and participate in sports. He did not simply preach *at* his congregation, either; he listened to them and treated them as individuals, with individual concerns and problems. "It wasn't so much what he did to help," Robinson would later recall, "as the fact that he was interested and concerned enough to offer the best advice he could."[9] A few years later, while Jackie was attending the University of California at Los Angeles (UCLA), he returned to the community on weekends to teach Sunday school as a volunteer.

Pasadena Junior College

After graduating from Muir Technical High School, Robinson enrolled at Pasadena Junior College in 1937. While tuition was very reasonable at Pasadena, there were few blacks on campus besides Jackie and some other athletes. At first Jackie struggled in the shadow of his brother Mack, who had attended the college a few years before. Mack had been a star in the 1936 Olympics in Berlin, finishing second to Jesse Owens in several track events.

Jesse Owens displays the gold medals he won in the 1936 Olympics. Robinson's brother Mack competed against Owens.

Uncle Jack at Pasadena

In his biography, Jackie Robinson, *Harvey Frommer talked to Robinson's sister Willa Mae Robinson and came away with a humorous anecdote about Jackie from his UCLA days:*

"'At one of the football games,' notes Willa Mae, 'my youngest son, Ronnie, who was then six, started to shout: "C'mon, Uncle Jack, c'mon, Uncle Jack." And soon the whole stadium was calling out: "C'mon, Uncle Jack, c'mon, Uncle Jack." I knew I was going to be in for it. Jack didn't like that kind of publicity.

'I said, "I couldn't help it. What was my Ronnie going to call you?" And Jack laughed. He had a real good laugh.'"

At Pasadena Junior College, Robinson continued to experience racism. His football coach, Tom Mallory, remembered that Jackie "was touchy about the racial issue. We didn't have too many black players on the team in those days. Some people would say they didn't want to play against 'the nigger'."[10]

Jackie's refusal to quit the playing field won him the respect of teammates time and time again throughout his athletic career. His teammates would be impressed with his ability and character, and they would back him up. Despite the racism directed toward him, Jackie was as aggressively competitive as ever and backed down from no one.

His career at Pasadena Junior College was remarkable. Jackie excelled in baseball, track, football, and tennis. In baseball, he was chosen as the all-Southern California shortstop, and he led all California junior college players in base stealing. In track he became the national junior college record holder in the broad jump with a leap of twenty-five feet, six-and-a-half inches.

The impact on those who viewed Jackie in action was profound. Yoshi Hasegawa, a friend from the neighborhood and fellow student at Pasadena Junior College, recalled that Jackie was "outstanding. He used to make ninety-nine-yard touchdown runs. I haven't seen a touchdown like that ever. The way the guy used to run! There isn't anything like it! He'd go zigzagging all the way down, and nobody could catch him. He had those crazy legs."[11] A Pasadena newspaper named Jackie Outstanding Athlete of the Year in 1938, and a local writer called him the most outstanding athlete in the history of the college.

Tom Mallory spoke for many who had contact with the young athlete during the Pasadena years:

He was a very fine athlete and a fine man, and it was a privilege to coach him in school. I can't say that I expected he would turn out as he did, but I wasn't terribly surprised, either. Jackie Robinson was the kind of athlete

A newsphoto of Jackie at his first UCLA football practice. He was expected to be a star player for the Bruins.

who comes along once in a lifetime. You get a kid like that who can do so many things on a football field and you are getting a kid who will make you look like a real smart football coach.[12]

UCLA

After two years at Pasadena, Robinson transferred to UCLA, which had offered him a partial scholarship. There he continued his record of excellence. He became the school's first four-letter athlete in UCLA history. He was the West Coast's highest scorer in basketball and UCLA's best broad jumper. In football he led the nation's ballcarriers in rushing and punt returns. He led all West Coast college players in basketball scoring during his junior and senior years.

Two events influenced Jackie's personal life at UCLA. The first was the sudden death of his older brother Frank in a motorcycle accident. The pain of the loss was hard to bear, and Jackie never talked about it in public. The second event did much to soothe his brother's death. Jackie met Rachel Isum through a mutual friend, and soon the two began dating. Rachel was impressed with Jackie for several reasons:

Too often in those days, black people were made ashamed of their appearance. Jack was never ashamed of being black. In fact, he did something few

Robinson was an all-conference basketball player for UCLA as well as a football and track star.

blacks ever did. He always wore a white shirt. It showed off his dark skin. Many blacks wore dark shirts or colored shirts so that their skin color would not be so noticeable. . . . Jack was very shy with girls, and he always thought a girl who talked to him at school was only being friendly because he was a big athlete. I didn't know anything about sports then. I just knew he was a nice young man and very handsome.[13]

They soon dated each other exclusively even though Jackie was busy with his schoolwork and his exploits on UCLA's athletic fields.

Robinson never graduated from UCLA. Desiring to help his mother and suffering from financial hardships himself, he quit school just weeks before graduation to become assistant athletic director with a National Youth Administration (NYA) work camp, which was designed to provide social and economic opportunities for disadvantaged children. Robinson's decision to work with the NYA had been influenced by his relationship with Carl Anderson years before. But soon after Robinson reported for work, the NYA was shut down by the government. World War II had begun in Europe, and funds were diverted to prepare for the possibility of America's involvement.

Jobless, Robinson jumped at the chance to play professional football when he was offered a modest contract in 1941. As a member of the Honolulu Bears, he played football on Sundays and worked the rest of the week at construction jobs to support himself and help his mother, back home in Pasadena. But Robinson, who always longed to be near home, began to suffer from homesickness. The season ended on December 5, 1941, and Robinson immediately jumped on a ship for the long journey to California across the Pacific Ocean. Two days later Japan launched a surprise attack on Pearl Harbor in Honolulu and America entered World War II. A few months later Robinson received a letter from the Army: he had been drafted.

The Segregated Military

Blacks had long been active in America's armed forces. Many blacks fought in the Mexican-American War, and later many fought in the Civil War. Blacks were a major force, too, in World War I. Despite their service, blacks were always discriminated against.

During the Civil War black soldiers fought for the North, but they were segregated from white soldiers. They also were paid less than half of what the whites were paid. There were few black officers, and most black units were commanded by

Like these Civil War soldiers eighty years before him, Robinson had to endure racial discrimination in the military.

On December 7, 1941, Japan's surprise attack on Pearl Harbor leaves American ships burning. Robinson had left Honolulu just two days before the assault that plunged the United States into World War II.

white officers who were hardly sympathetic to them. Black soldiers were also given inferior equipment and medical attention.

During World War I black soldiers were subjected to harrowing conditions, especially at home. At Camp Hill in Virginia during the winter of 1917–1918, blacks preparing to fight overseas lived in tents with little or no heat or blankets, and with hardly any medical attention, the death rate was high.

During World War II blacks continued to experience the same racism in the military. In the navy blacks performed only menial jobs, such as cleaning latrines and working in the commissary. The air force was reluctant in the early years of the war to accept black pilots, even those who had had experience in the Spanish Civil War. The army was no different from the other branches of service when it came to racism against blacks. Black soldiers suffered from segregation on military bases and had to defer to white soldiers in such simple matters as boarding a bus or using a telephone.

Most blacks in the military quietly accepted their second-class status. They understood that their uniforms gave them a measure of self-respect and authority; they appreciated that they were being fed, clothed, and housed; and they were glad to be learning trades and skills otherwise unattainable in civilian life. They were ready and willing to fight against the Japanese in the Pacific and the racist ideologies of the Nazis in Europe. But privately most blacks "could not understand why whites drew distinctions between the Nazi ideology of Aryan supremacy and the American ideology of white supremacy."[14]

Black soldiers land on shore during World War II. Despite heroic service, few blacks in Robinson's day could hope to become officers.

Fort Riley

Shortly after his arrival at Fort Riley, Kansas, Robinson was made aware of his inferior status as a black soldier. He hoped to join the baseball team but was told bluntly that Negro players were not wanted. The football team invited him to play, but a pass to visit his mother was suddenly urged upon him just before the season began. It was obvious that military officials did not want to see him on the playing field, and Robinson, disgusted with this kind of treatment, quit the team.

In the spring of 1942 Robinson applied for officer candidate training. The application was rejected. He applied again, and again he was refused. Each time, the same rationale for rejection appeared on the application: "He is not a leader of men." But it was clear that this reason was not the issue: blacks were not to be permitted to enter Fort Riley's Officer Candidate School

(OCS). There were, in fact, black officers in the army, but most of them had been trained at northern posts.

Then Robinson got a lucky break. Joe Louis, the world heavyweight boxing champion, was transferred to Fort Riley. Louis's army responsibilities included talking about boxing to the troops and entertaining them with boxing exhibitions. When Robinson told Louis about the rejection of his OCS applications, the boxing great called Washington, D.C., and explained to a contact there that Robinson was being categorically refused. The call was a success for Robinson, who remembered that immediately afterwards Fort Riley "began to get some heat from Washington and we [blacks] suddenly found ourselves being welcomed into OCS."[15]

After becoming an officer, Robinson continued to object to segregation. In January 1943 Robinson's first duty as second lieutenant was to be the morale officer of a black unit; it was his job to listen to the

Rachel Remembers

In his book on the Brooklyn Dodgers called Bums, *Peter Golenbock interviews Robinson's wife Rachel:*

"When I met Jackie, he had already established somewhat of a reputation. He was a letterman in four sports. He was very famous on campus and in the area because UCLA had good teams in those days. He was known as a football star and a basketball star. He was not known in baseball at all, and he held a broad jump record. And he won some local tennis tournaments. The only thing he didn't do was swim.

Jackie never concentrated on track. He probably could have gone to the Olympics. He was really concentrating on football and basketball. When he left school, he didn't want to be a professional football player for any length of time because he had already had some permanent injuries as a result of it. He had bone chips in his ankle, which couldn't be removed, so he didn't think he wanted to be a professional football player.

After going to [Pasadena Junior College] for two years, he played sports two years at UCLA and then he lost interest in school once he had used up his athletic eligibility and couldn't play. The university encouraged him to stay on and finish and get his degree, but he was concerned that his mother had worked long enough and hard enough, and his brothers were in college, and they felt they needed to get out and start helping her.

Robinson at UCLA.

So he quit school and took a job with a National Youth Administration work camp, working with youngsters. When [World War II] broke out, the government closed the camp, and when he was laid off from that he made some money with the Honolulu Bears in football. . . . Jackie was on his way home from Honolulu to Los Angeles the day Pearl Harbor was bombed. They blacked out the ship. After Pearl Harbor, Jackie went into the service for thirty-six months."

Boxing great Joe Louis used his clout in Washington to open the door of Officer Candidate School for Robinson.

The major was not enthusiastic about Robinson's idea. He informed Robinson curtly that segregation was policy and custom in the PX. Blacks were not welcome to sit wherever they pleased. Assuming that the man he was speaking to was white, the major tried his own brand of reasoning with Robinson: "How would you like to have your wife sitting next to a nigger?"

Robinson, of course, wanted to hang up, find the provost marshal, and beat the daylights out of him. Instead, he tore into the other man verbally. "I was so angry that I asked him if he knew how close his wife had ever been to a nigger," recalled Robinson. "I was shouting at the top of my voice. Every typewriter in headquarters stopped. The clerks were frozen in disbelief at the way I ripped into the major."[16]

Fortunately, another army official heard Robinson's tirade. A Colonel Longley's office was nearby, and Robinson was quickly summoned to explain what had

While in the army, Jackie Robinson fought and won many battles against segregation and discrimination.

men and try to solve their problems. And it was by trying to integrate the post exchange, or PX, that he gained first-hand experience of difficulties blacks faced throughout the country. The PX was a store on the military base where the soldiers could make phone calls, pick up their mail, or have a bite to eat.

The men in his unit were depressed over the regulations they faced at the segregated PX. Only half a dozen seats were designated for blacks, so Robinson and other black soldiers had to stand in line, waiting to use them, while numerous whites-only tables went unused. Some of his men complained at the unequal treatment. Even though they risked their lives for their country, they could not get the same service that white soldiers enjoyed at the PX.

Robinson soon contacted the provost marshal, a Major Hafner. Speaking over the telephone, the young lieutenant explained the situation that hurt the morale of his men and told Hafner that segregation in the PX should be eliminated.

happened. The colonel listened to Robinson's explanation and agreed to help. A few days later the base's commanding general received a strong letter from Colonel Longley, demanding that conditions at the PX be changed. Longley also recommended that the provost marshal be disciplined for his racist language. "I have always been grateful to Colonel Longley," Robinson said in his later years. "He proved to me that when people in authority take a stand, good can come out of it." [17]

Fort Hood

Perhaps because of this incident, Robinson was soon transferred to Fort Hood, Texas, where his career in the army would come to an abrupt end. At first things went well for Robinson at Fort Hood. Displaying his leadership abilities as the head of a tank battalion, Robinson made a strong impression on his commanding officer; in fact, the officer asked Robinson to go overseas with him as morale officer. "He said that . . . I was able to get the best out of people I worked with," Robinson later recalled. [18] In order to go overseas Robinson had to submit to a health examination and testing at an army hospital some thirty miles from the base.

Once at the hospital, Robinson went through several tests, then was told that the examination would resume in a day or two. He decided to go back to the base to visit friends at the officers' club. Finding them gone on maneuvers, he boarded a military bus to make a connection with the city bus that would return him to the hospital. He recognized the light-skinned wife of one of the other black officers and sat beside her at the middle of the bus. Suddenly the driver of the bus started yelling for Robinson to move to the back.

A Change in Voting Strategy

Langston Hughes, Milton Meltzer, and Eric C. Lincoln collaborated on a fine work called A Pictorial History of Black Americans. *In this excerpt the authors write about Roosevelt's New Deal programs, which employed many blacks:*

"The various governmental agencies which were set up to cope with the problems brought by the depression aided Negroes culturally, as well as in terms of sustenance. The Works Projects Administration, the National Youth Administration, the Civilian Conservation Corps camps, the Federal Theater [opened up] jobs to them from which private industry had excluded them. No wonder Negroes called F. D. R. the 'Great White Father' and when he ran again for President in 1936, voted almost overwhelmingly Democratic. In 1934 Arthur W. Mitchell, the first Negro Democrat ever in Congress, was elected from Chicago."

Unlike Robinson eleven years before her, Rosa Parks (right) made history when she was arrested for refusing to sit at the back of a Montgomery, Alabama, city bus in 1955. Her arrest led to a U.S. Supreme Court decision banning segregation on public transit.

"Listen you," the driver shouted, "I said get to the back of the bus where colored people belong."

"Now you listen to me," Robinson responded, "you just drive the bus and I'll sit where I please."

Eleven years later Rosa Parks, a Montgomery, Alabama, seamstress, would refuse to sit in the back of a city bus. Her refusal to leave and subsequent arrest led to a one-day boycott by black·Montgomery residents and, in effect, started the movement for civil rights in the South. In 1944, however, Jackie Robinson was not riding the wave of the civil rights movement. He was all alone.

At the post bus's last stop, Robinson stepped off at the front. The driver dashed down the steps after him and ran for help. Two military policemen at the post gate listened to the irate driver, then approached Robinson and escorted him to the office of the duty officer, Captain Gerald Bear. Meanwhile, the driver had already given Bear's secretary his version of the incident.

The captain sat back while his secretary related the driver's story and accused Robinson of trying to start a race riot. Robinson stated that the only thing he was trying to do was return to the hospital. Bear's secretary apparently took offense at Robinson's remarks. She accused him of being a troublemaker because he knew he wasn't supposed to sit where he had. When Robinson told her that he was just trying to enjoy his rights, he was verbally attacked by the captain.

Years later Robinson would recall the encounter: "Captain Bear came out of hibernation to growl that I was apparently an uppity nigger and that I had no right to speak to that lady in that manner."[19]

Robinson was ordered back to the hospital to await military trial for insubordination. The case went to military court, where the charges were as ridiculous and ugly as some of the comments that had been made by Captain Bear and his secretary. Robinson stood before the court while the prosecuting attorney accused him of disturbing the peace, disobeying an order, acting with disrespect toward a civilian woman, and, as Robinson later recalled, "of contemptuously bowing, giving sloppy salutes to Captain Bear and repeating several times, 'Okay, sir. Okay, sir.'"[20]

Two Wars

In his biography, Jackie Robinson: First of the Chosen Few, *Joseph Nazel briefly outlines the ambivalence many blacks felt about fighting in World War II for a country that discriminated against them. He describes how Robinson responded to this:*

"The news [of Pearl Harbor] stunned Jackie. No matter what the conditions were at home, he was an American. And he, like many young black Americans, would be tattered by haunting questions. Could they fight for a country that denied them basic human rights? And if they fought, would it change things? Would they have proven their right to be treated equally?

It was a traumatic time for black Americans who had not as yet resolved the conflict of their two warring factions—Negro vs. American. Would they fight?

[Black sailor] Dorie Miller had already distinguished himself by manning a gun in defense of his ship during the Japanese attack on Pearl Harbor. He had not been trained to fight or to use the weapon he used to shoot down four Japanese fighters. In earning the Navy Cross he had proven that black Americans were not only ready to fight but could fight. He was neither promoted nor moved to a more challenging post.

The war should have provided that common ground between black and white Americans. Blacks were ready to settle the issues and get on about the war. Jackie Robinson would write later, 'I felt there were two wars raging at once—one against foreign enemies and one against domestic foes—and the black man was forced to fight both. . . . It isn't a perfect America and it isn't run right,' Jackie concluded, 'but it still belongs to us.' By 1942 Jackie Robinson was serving in the United States Army."

Robinson's lawyer made a persuasive case. He contended that the articles of war had not been violated and, therefore, Robinson did not deserve a court-martial on the grounds of insubordination. The lawyer concluded by arguing that the real threat to the military was quite minimal, but that a few people were "working vengeance against an uppity black man."[21]

The charges against Robinson were dropped. Nonetheless, his reputation as a troublemaker was reinforced—but he had fought, and he had won. Fed up with the service, he wrote a letter to the adjutant general, a top army official, in Washington, D.C., complaining of his treatment. Robinson gambled on the adjutant general's deciding that Robinson was too much of a troublemaker and that the army would be better off without him. The gamble paid off. Jackie was suddenly transferred from Texas in November 1944 to Fort Breckenridge, Kentucky, to receive a medical discharge. Obviously some people at the top wanted the troublemaker out!

Before he left the army, though, an incident occurred that gave an interesting prelude to Robinson's future. While Robinson was walking across a baseball field in Texas just before his transfer to Fort Breckenridge, someone hit a ball that rolled right up to his feet. He picked up the stray ball, spied the outfielder far away, reared back, and fired a perfect strike right into the man's glove. A man from the group approached him and asked Robinson if he'd like to play baseball professionally. Robinson took the man's phone number, put it in his pocket, and walked away. Little did he know that he would call this number and take his first step toward a professional baseball career when the man would sign him up with the Kansas City Monarchs.

2 Rickey and Robinson

The first baseball organization was formed in 1859 in the United States. This organization, the National Association of Baseball Players, was made up of more than one hundred teams. Blacks were allowed to play, but mostly in the northeast and southeast. Though this arrangement allowed blacks to play alongside whites, blacks were not treated fairly, and they always feared physical violence. Former sports broadcaster and NBC-TV talk show host Art Rust Jr., notes that "Negro infielders wore shin guards because white opponents would try to spike them at every opportunity. Pitchers aimed at their heads."[22]

Two years after the end of the Civil War, however, the baseball organization changed its policy toward blacks. In December 1867, at its annual convention in Philadelphia, the National Association of Baseball Players decided to bar blacks and clubs that allowed them to play. Art Rust notes that this organization's successor, the National Association of Professional Baseball Players, formed in 1871, "never had a written rule against black players, but there existed a 'gentlemen's agreement' barring blacks from this first professional league and its successor, the National League."[23]

Prohibited from playing in the white professional leagues in the late 1800s, blacks organized their own teams and leagues, which survived into the next century. "There was no secret why the black leagues started and why they endured," continues Rust. "They started because white players threatened to quit rather than share the diamond with black men."[24] Many leagues had come and gone by the time the Negro National League, the first black professional league, was created in 1920 by Rube Foster, a former black baseball star who had managed several black teams. The Negro National League soon spawned several other professional leagues, including the Negro American League and the Eastern League.

The action heats up in a Negro League baseball game in 1943. Many black players in this league could have had noteworthy careers in the major leagues.

Outstanding Negro League infielder Buck Leonard tags out a New York Cubans base runner. The Negro leagues often lost their best players to better offers from foreign baseball leagues.

By the 1940s the Negro leagues, the Negro National League and the Negro American League, each had six teams. These teams had names like the Baltimore Elite Giants, the Kansas City Monarchs, and the New York Cubans. Many great black ballplayers graced the fields of the Negro leagues and, as Art Rust contends,

> if given the chance, could have made it in the majors and earned five-figure salaries. There was Josh Gibson of the Pittsburgh Crawfords. He certainly could have made it. Black ballplayers said he could hit the ball a ton. And there was Cool Papa Bell of the St. Louis Stars, an outfielder as speedy and graceful as Tris Speaker. And then there was a pitcher, Leroy "Satchel" Paige, who did for black baseball what Babe Ruth did for white baseball.[25]

Even the best ballplayers, though, suffered from instability and uncertainty. As Rust states:

Schedules in the Negro leagues were irregular, and games were vulnerable to sudden cancellation. Players were always jumping teams for richer offers in Mexico and other Latin leagues. Only the black equivalent of the All-Star Game, the East-West Game, was a sure success, drawing as many as fifty-one thousand fans to Chicago's Comiskey Park in 1943.[26]

Art Rust summarizes life for the ballplayers of the Negro leagues:

> Organized black teams played full schedules in their own leagues, despite substandard wages, abominable playing conditions, and poor transportation. The black man played ball in preference to taking the miserable jobs offered him elsewhere.[27]

The black ballplayers' pay was low. In the 1940s at the height of the leagues'

Pitcher Leroy "Satchel" Paige was the Babe Ruth of the Negro League.

Dodgers great Roy Campanella reaches for a fly ball. Campanella came to the Brooklyn team from the Negro League.

Road accommodations usually ranged from the uncomfortable to the uninhabitable. Most major hotels were segregated. . . . In areas where no facilities for blacks existed, ballplayers slept on the bus or outside at the ball park. The average black hotel of that era also lacked appeal. "We were continually under attack by bedbugs," says [Quincy] Trouppe. "My roomie and I stayed up many nights in Pittsburgh fighting these monsters until morning."

When critics censured Negro league owners for the poor housing, Effa Manley, the co-owner of the Newark Eagles, responded that owners lacked the power to rectify the situation. "Until Congress makes statutory changes on race prejudice in hotels," she argued, "I'm afraid there's little we can do to better such accommodations."[29]

Many in the Negro leagues were philosophical about their second-class status. Roy Campanella, the future Dodger great, stated that many ballplayers came from inner-city slums and that "a Negro ball player, playing Negro ball in the United States, might not have lived like a king, but he didn't live bad either." Another Negro league catcher, Quincy Trouppe, declared that "baseball opened doors for me" and that "because of this great national game, I have lived a life comparable to the wealthiest man in the United States."[30]

prosperity, the very best players received about $500 a month. They also faced much more grueling schedules than white players. They traveled from town to town packed into cars or shuttled onto buses. Roy Campanella remembered his days with the Baltimore Elite Giants: "We traveled in a big bus and many's the time we never bothered to take off our uniforms going from one place to another. . . . The bus was our home, dressing room, dining room, and hotel."[28]

Accommodations were especially hard to bear. Jules Tygiel, in his book *Baseball's Great Experiment,* states:

The Need for Integration

It was inevitable that blacks would soon enter major league baseball. Beginning in 1943 determined efforts were begun to integrate baseball. In that year segregation was officially banned by the reigning baseball commissioner, Kenesaw Landis. However, it was common knowledge that Landis had caved in to pressure from newspaper columnists around the country and was secretly in favor of keeping blacks out. Bill Veeck, then the owner of a club in the minor leagues, planned to buy the Philadelphia Phillies that year and hire only blacks to compete against the white teams of the major leagues. When Veeck informed Landis of his idea, the baseball commissioner allegedly made some secret phone calls and arranged the sale of the Phillies to a Philadelphia businessman, who paid half the price Veeck was prepared to pay, thus dashing Veeck's plan.

Also in 1943 Clark Griffith, the owner of the Washington Senators, almost signed several black players. But after the players agreed to a deal, Griffith could think only of the problems involved—where would they eat, and where would they sleep? How would the other players feel about them? He could not answer these questions, and the deal fell through.

Baseball commissioner Keneshaw Landis throws out the season's first ball. Landis officially banned segregation in 1943.

But the time seemed right. Throughout the United States blacks were fighting determinedly for equality. Race riots in Harlem, Detroit, and in Beaumont, Texas, in 1943 proved that blacks were willing to fight for their rights. President Franklin D. Roosevelt's recent creation of the Fair Employment Practices Committee, which supervised discrimination practices in employment, proved that the government was listening.

Two men stare in disbelief at a sign segregating a Jackson, Mississippi, railway station in 1955. When the railroad ended its segregation policy, the city established one in order to continue segregation at the station.

Despite police protection, a black man is assaulted by a white man during a 1943 race riot in Detroit.

As writer Jules Tygiel points out, there were two other factors in America's concern with integration immediately after the war: "a small coterie of young black sportswriters and the Communist Party, one of the few groups concerned with civil rights issues during the depression years."[31] The small but influential group of black journalists was led by Wendell Smith, Sam Lacy, and Joe Bostic. Their columns on racism and discrimination in sports appeared in the nation's largest newspapers and made fans across the nation aware of the problems of prejudice.

The other factor was the Communist Party of the United States. While never a strong force for change in American politics, the Communist Party spoke out loudly on many issues in the thirties and forties, including racism in baseball—America's national pastime. Articles of protest appeared regularly in the organization's newspaper, *The Daily Worker*. On opening day of the 1945 baseball season, the Communist Party held a protest march outside Yankee Stadium in New York.

Branch Rickey

In 1945, at the end of World War II, Branch Rickey saw that things were about to change and he wanted to be the first to make it happen. Rickey loved baseball. Born December 20, 1881, in Stockdale, Ohio, he played and coached baseball in college at Ohio Wesleyan, then went on to play as a catcher in the major leagues. After

Dodgers general manager Branch Rickey chose Jackie Robinson as the first black to play in the major leagues.

Monte Irvin entered the majors soon after Jackie Robinson. Irvin credited Branch Rickey with making his advancement possible.

his playing career ended he became involved in baseball management and developed scouting and farm systems for several major league clubs. The Brooklyn Dodgers hired him as their general manager in 1942.

Rickey knew how to produce winning baseball teams. According to author Jeffrey Hart, Rickey made long-range plans for a ball club. "He liked to assemble a talented crew of players of approximately the same age and plan for a decade or more of service from them."[32] Up through and including the years of American involvement in World War II, none of the players on the teams Rickey had assembled for the major leagues had been black.

Rickey's Decision

Branch Rickey had several reasons for wanting to bring the first black man to baseball's major leagues. Besides simply loving a challenge, Rickey wanted to show

up his contemporaries—the other baseball executives. When he discussed with them the prospect of a black man in baseball, they all scoffed at him. It was not the right time to bring a black man into baseball, they insisted. Rickey wanted to prove them wrong. Monte Irvin, a black ballplayer who came into the major leagues shortly after Robinson, explained Rickey's contribution: "It took Branch Rickey to come up with the answers, to do it."[33]

For Rickey, there was also the prospect of profiting from such a venture. Rickey knew full well that blacks across the country who knew nothing about baseball would turn out in droves at the local ball parks to see one of their own compete against whites in the big leagues. They would be entitled to fill the stadiums if they wanted, for the long-standing laws segregating baseball stands had been abolished in 1944.

Finally, Rickey wanted a place in history. To others and to himself, Rickey was a bit larger than the game of baseball. He was an intellectual man who felt he had a moral purpose in life, a duty to make the world better than he found it—and he wanted to be remembered. While scouting for the right man to be the first black in baseball, Rickey confided to an associate that, after witnessing racism against blacks, "I decided that if I ever had the opportunity I was going to do something for the Negro race. . . . Now I am ready!"[34] Writer Maury Allen describes him as "a flamboyant figure . . . a religious mystic and loquacious, sometimes convoluted, speaker—an orator, if the occasion moved him, of overwhelming skills."[35]

After meeting with the owners of the Dodgers in 1943 and getting their approval, he began his search for a black ballplayer.

Looking For Something Permanent

In Bums, *Peter Golenbock interviews Rachel Robinson about the time before it was clear that Jackie would have a steady future with the Dodgers:*

"The Monarchs, for Jackie, were never talked about as something permanent. He always talked about it as making extra money until he could settle down into something, till we got married and knew what we were going to do. So I doubt very much whether he would have put up with that for very long. It just wasn't his style. It was terrible for a person like him, because a lot of their games were played in the South, and it was a constant holding back, controlling yourself under those circumstances, but in those days, there was absolutely no choice. But because he played for the Monarchs that year, he eventually got his chance with the Dodgers. There's something about destiny in that somewhere, I think.

I remember when he had the meeting with Rickey, Jack called me. He said it was very secret and he couldn't tell me a lot over the telephone. He really didn't appreciate the magnitude of it at that point. He just saw it as an opportunity, as something exciting, and that he would have a chance. When he called, he told me he would be going to Montreal, and that's about it.

Mr. Rickey was the one very concerned about the preparation. He really thought the preparation was extremely important to the success of the venture. So he laid out the groundwork in Brooklyn. He fixed us up with a family in [Bedford-Stuyvesant]. He saw them as a family we could turn to for things. Very community-minded people and very warm, generous, and loving people, and they became our second family. He made the first contact for us long before we even came to Brooklyn."

Branch Rickey considered Negro League star Ray Dandridge too old to be the first black player in the majors.

A Symbol Needed

Rickey thought hard about the type of black man necessary to integrate baseball. He decided the man had to become a symbol, someone to whom blacks and whites alike could easily relate and yet see as a larger-than-life figure. Rickey knew that black Americans needed a black American in the public eye, a symbol on whom they could pin their hopes and dreams.

This symbol had to have several important attributes. Branch Rickey knew that there had to be no doubt about the person's skin color—that was crucial. Writer Maury Allen asserts that the black player's bloodlines could have "no white skeletons in the woodshed. This appealed strongly to the moralistic side of Rickey. It would also eliminate the reverse discrimination of some people suggesting that a lighter-skinned black had mixed ancestry and was trying to pass for white."[36]

The man also had to fully realize and understand and support his identity as a symbol; he had to be actively involved in breaking down color barriers in baseball, as well as educated enough to express himself clearly and directly. Because the first black ballplayer would be scrutinized daily in the public spotlight, he had to be very tough-minded. He had to be able to handle the media pressure.

The man also needed to be tough enough to carry out the strategy of nonviolent resistance; that is, he had to understand and use the tactic of standing up for one's rights without using physical force or threats. He had to focus not on black power but on justice.

Finally, the man had to be an excellent ballplayer. This was very important, because if he failed on the ball field, the claim would be that blacks were simply not good enough to play with whites.

Rickey looked in the Negro leagues for the man he needed. On a list composed by his scouts, Rickey had the names of nearly a dozen players, including Roy Campanella, Judy Johnson, Cool Papa Bell,

Judy Johnson was considered, but rejected, as Rickey's choice for the first black player to enter the major leagues.

Talented Josh Gibson's personal problems took him out of the running for major league baseball's first black player.

Satchel Paige, Monte Irvin, Josh Gibson, Buck Leonard, Ray Dandridge—and a newcomer named Jackie Robinson.

After looking carefully into the lives of the men whose names were written on his list, Rickey crossed many of them off. Josh Gibson, it was discovered, had a drinking problem. Satchel Paige was reported to have a difficult temperament; people said he was hard to handle. Buck Leonard, Cool Papa Bell, and Ray Dandridge were too old. Roy Campanella was an outstanding player— but did he have the guts to take all the abuse he would meet up with from white bigots? Rickey wasn't so sure. All names were finally crossed off the list—but one.

Jackie Robinson appeared to be the right man for the job. His skin color was undeniably black. He was educated and well-spoken, so he could express his thoughts clearly to the press. He believed firmly in civil rights and had fought over these issues in an acceptable manner before, so he had enough mental toughness to be able to turn the other cheek. Last, and most importantly, he was a fine ballplayer. With his college education, com-

petitiveness, his notable Olympian brother Mack—and of course his all-around ability—Robinson became Rickey's choice.

Rickey proceeded carefully. He did not want his plan open to criticism by having it exposed and he told no one, not even his closest friends, of the reasons behind his scouting efforts. When asked by the press why his scouts were watching black ballplayers, he explained that he was recruiting players for the Brooklyn Brown Dodgers, a new team in the new black league he planned to establish. Of course, this was simply a ruse. Rickey knew the value of holding a story until the very last minute for maximum impact. He wanted the public to be jolted by the signing of Robinson. He wanted attention to be fixed on Robinson while he made the dream of integration in baseball come true.

Robinson in the Negro Leagues

In 1945 Jackie Robinson was playing in the Negro leagues for the Kansas City Monarchs. He had returned to Pasadena after his army experience and had an offer to coach football at a small black college, but the Monarchs offered him more money. His brother Mack encouraged him to take the job.

Robinson was having a tough time with the Monarchs. Although he was named to the All-Star team at midseason and would end up with a strong .340 batting average, for much of the season he played back-up shortstop. He did not mix well with other players, either: while many drank and partied, Robinson, a nondrinker and nonsmoker, complained of their lack of discipline.

We Were Entertainers

Roy Campanella and Robinson were miles apart, in terms of temperament. But they shared many of the same experiences—including life in the Negro leagues. In his autobiography, It's Good to Be Alive, *Campanella looks back with fondness at his days with the Baltimore Elite Giants:*

"A Negro ballplayer, playing Negro ball in the States, might not have lived like a king, but he didn't live bad, either. Actually, with the Elites, we were never in any one town long enough to think about the poor side of cities. Sure we knew it was there. . . . As a matter of fact we had a lot of players in both leagues who had come from slum neighborhoods of big towns. Playing ball was a way to beat that, to move on to something better.

After all, we were entertainers. We were out there to give the paying customers a show. I don't mean the sort of clowning that the Harlem Globetrotters put on with their basketball, we just played as good as we knew how.

And we were always wanted for exhibition games when we were on the road—games against both white and colored teams. We had some great players, and those white semi-pro clubs used to really bear down against us."

Roy Campanella had fond memories of his pre-Dodgers days in the Negro League.

Segregation infuriated Jackie Robinson when he encountered it during his Negro League career.

Most disturbing to Robinson, though, was the racism the Monarchs encountered wherever they went. He had a hard time controlling his temper whenever he and his teammates received second-class treatment. Jules Tygiel learned that one of Robinson's teammates on the Kansas City Monarchs, Othello Renfroe, had trouble with Robinson's attitude, especially when the team bus "pulled up in service stations in Mississippi where drinking fountains said black and white and couple of times we had to leave without our change, he'd get so mad."[37]

The Historic Meeting

If Robinson infuriated his Negro leagues teammates, he genuinely pleased Branch Rickey, who sent Dodgers scout Clyde Sukeforth to meet with him in Chicago. Sukeforth talked briefly to Robinson at the stadium and asked him to meet him that night at his hotel. Sukeforth remembered that evening well:

Before I went up to my room I told the doorman a colored man would be coming by later to see me and to let him up to my room. I gave him a few bucks, and he said he would. I can't remember what time it was but I think it was about midnight when Robinson knocked on the door of my room. I opened it up and let him in. He was a wonderful-looking athlete, a very good-looking man, with those big, broad shoulders and large hands. I think he was wearing a gray sports jacket and gray slacks.

We sat down to talk about his baseball ability and the fact that Mr. Rickey wanted to meet with him personally. He had a very distinct voice, very cultured, and chose his words carefully. Determination was written all over his face. This wasn't a young man who would be pushed around. It wasn't hard to tell he was a highly intelligent man. I was very impressed.[38]

The next day Sukeforth and Robinson were on their way by train to New York for Robinson's meeting with the Dodgers' owner.

Dodgers scout Clyde Sukeforth first met with Jackie Robinson about joining the Brooklyn club. He recalled being very impressed with the young black player.

They met in Rickey's office. Rickey sat behind his desk and motioned for Robinson to sit, too. Robinson complied, and the two men faced one another. There was silence. Not a word was said for several minutes while Rickey stared at Robinson and Robinson stared back, wondering what was going on. He later learned that Rickey would regularly act this way with an individual who intrigued him—it was just his way of "getting inside" a person.

Finally, Rickey spoke. "You were brought here to play for the Brooklyn organization, to start out, if you can make it, playing for our top farm team, the Montreal Royals." Robinson took a deep breath, and Rickey continued:

> I want to win pennants. We need ballplayers. We have scouted you for weeks. What you can do on the baseball field is a matter of record. But this is much more than just playing baseball, much more. What I mean when I say "can you make it" is do you have the guts, do you have the guts and what it takes to make it?

Robinson had a hard time accepting Rickey at his word. It was just too fantastic to be true. He was wary, but as Rickey began to talk about how it would be for Robinson that first season, Robinson let his guard down.

Rickey continued:

> There is virtually no group on our side. No umpires, no club owners, maybe a few newspapermen. We will be in a very tough spot. I have a great fear that there will be some fans who will be highly hostile to what we are doing. Jackie, it will be a tough position to be in, an almost impossible position. But we can win if we can convince everyone that you are

not only a great ballplayer but also a great gentleman. . . . We have no army, no soldiers. Our weapons will be base hits and stolen bases and swallowed pride. Those will do the job and get the victory—that's what will win . . . and Jackie, nothing, nothing else will do it.[39]

To prepare Robinson for what he would face, Rickey described the most uncomfortable situations and used the most graphic language. "Beanballs would be thrown at me," Robinson said, recalling the conversation. "I would be called the kind of names which would hurt and infuriate any man. I would be physically attacked."[40] Robinson had a hard time hearing this. "His acting was so convincing," he recalled, "that I found myself chain-gripping my fingers behind my back."[41]

In his autobiography, *I Never Had It Made*, Robinson recalled what else went

---

Everybody Can Understand Business

In his biography of Robinson, A Life Remembered, *Maury Allen interviews Mack Robinson, Jackie's older brother as he recalled the news of Jackie's signing to the Dodgers:*

"I remember when Branch Rickey first signed Jack and we all said 'What's this all about?' We didn't really think it was for the big leagues. There had been all that talk about a black team in Brooklyn. Jack said, 'No sir, this is a chance to make the big league Brooklyn Dodgers.' It was exciting.

Why did Rickey sign him? That was business, clear and simple. He wanted a black player because he thought it would help the Brooklyn club win and he thought it would bring people into the ballpark.

Everybody can understand business. I think what was more important, why I admire Rickey, is that he had the guts to do it. A lot of them were talking about having a black in the game but only Rickey did it. He stuck his neck out. He could have had it chopped off like one of those chickens we have out in the backyard. But he did it. Jack was the right man and did the job.

Jack wasn't all that certain he could make it. He used to call out here on the phone, and he would say it was awful rough and people were writing him nasty letters and he was scared for his life a good part of the time. But he was a strong fellow, very determined, and if anybody could make it, Jack was the one."

---

through his mind while Rickey was speaking, and how Rickey responded to an urgent question:

> He knew I would have terrible problems and wanted me to know the extent of them before I agreed to the plan. I was twenty-six years old, and all my life back to the age of eight when a little neighbor girl called me a nigger—I had believed in payback, retaliation. The most luxurious possession, the richest treasure anybody has, is his personal dignity. I looked at Mr. Rickey guardedly, and in that second I was looking at him not as a partner in a great experiment, but as the enemy—a white man. I had a question and it was the age-old one about whether or not you sell your birthright.
>
> "Mr. Rickey," I asked, "are you looking for a Negro who is afraid to fight back?"
>
> I will never forget the way he exploded.
>
> "Robinson," he said, "I'm looking for a ballplayer with guts enough not to fight back!"[42]

Rickey went on to explain how Robinson had to refuse to fight back. He had to turn the other cheek to taunts and threats. He had to prove himself as a capable ballplayer without resorting to the violence of the mudslingers.

Robinson took in all the information and thought for several minutes. There was no question about his feelings about staying in the Negro leagues. Said Robinson in later years, "if Mr. Rickey hadn't signed me, I wouldn't have played another year in the black league. It was too difficult. The travel was brutal. Financially, there was no reward. It took everything you made to live off."[43]

After a long silence, Robinson gave his decision. He agreed to accept the challenge. He promised there would be no violence—no retaliation on his part—during his tenure with the Dodgers. He signed a contract and left the office, sworn to secrecy until Rickey told him he could reveal the news. Rickey wanted to orchestrate the announcement himself, for maximum impact.

On October 23, 1945, a surprise press conference was held in Montreal announcing the signing of Jackie Robinson by the Brooklyn Dodgers organization. As Jules Tygiel recalls, "a moment of 'stunned silence' ensued before the reporters dashed for telephones to relate the startling story to their newspapers and radio stations."[44] The news spread fast all over America.

Rickey announced that Robinson, who stood by his side "nervous as the devil," would play in the International League, perhaps the best of several minor leagues in the country. He would play in Montreal for the Royals, Brooklyn's top farm team for young and developing talent. With its bilingual population and sophisticated media, Montreal was a world away from other International League cities, like Jersey City, Newark, and Buffalo. The city would provide a comfortable setting in which Robinson could prove himself worthy of promotion to the Dodgers.

Robinson, looking out at the sea of reporters, smiled confidently. To the reporters, he said only, "I'm ready to take the chance. Maybe I'm doing something for my race."[45] He certainly was doing something for his race. But he would have a very tough year ahead of him in which to prove it.

3 A Difficult Strategy

Robinson's appointment to the Montreal Royals was just part of a sweeping movement in America of black economic and political improvement in the mid-1940s. In his book, *The Shaping of Black America,* Lerone Bennett Jr., states that with World War II's winding down, black soldiers began returning to their cities and hometowns and made an impact on the economy:

> The war years changed the occupational profile of the black community and brought a dramatic increase in the number of black technicians and white-collar workers. This change, in turn, stimulated the real estate market and created new opportunities for realtors, financiers, and advertisers.[46]

In the political sphere, attitudes at the highest levels of government were changing. In his first year as president in 1945, Harry S Truman appointed a black lawyer to the United States Customs Court and nominated William H. Hastie, also black, for the governorship of the American Virgin Islands. In 1946 Truman instructed the Department of Justice to look into murders of blacks in Georgia and to investigate mob violence in general. Also in that year he issued a very profound executive order, creating the President's Committee on Civil Rights "to study, report and recommend 'effective means and procedures for the protection of the civil rights of the people of the United States.'"[47] In 1947, at the Lincoln Memorial in Washington, Truman became the first president ever to speak publicly to an NAACP conference.

Robinson's rise to the majors was part of a nationwide movement toward equality. This aircraft worker is one of thousands of blacks whose job status improved markedly after World War II.

Jackie Robinson adds another stolen base to his impressive statistics as a Montreal Royal.

The Impact of the First Black Ballplayer

Coming at the start of such changes, having a black ballplayer in the major leagues would make a tremendous impact on black and white Americans alike. Blacks who knew nothing about baseball would suddenly be drawn into the very public drama of a black person's struggling against the odds to make good in an area dominated solely by whites. Blacks would root proudly for his success—and for their own. White America, aware of the efforts of its black servicemen in World War II,

would have the chance to make good on its past wrongs and take steps to ensure the full integration of blacks into American society. White Americans would have the opportunity to learn that blacks were like anyone else. They would see that black Americans, represented by a single black athlete struggling to succeed, were worthy of respect and fair treatment.

That is, if he succeeded. For the first black ballplayer, the opportunity for failure would be ever present. He would constantly be in the public eye, insulted and discriminated against everywhere he went. He would have the double burden of being required to play excellent ball and

Torment and Torture

Duke Snider was the Dodgers center fielder and a close friend of Robinson's. In his book, The Duke of Flatbush, *he recalls the terrible torment Robinson had to endure while playing in the major leagues:*

"'Torment' seems almost too mild a word to describe what Jackie went through. 'Torture' would be more like it. He had promised Mr. Rickey there would be no incidents, after Mr. Rickey told him he wanted a black player who had the courage not to fight back. Right from the start of his rookie season all the way through his first year, and for years after that, Jackie endured what no other mere mortal could or should.

The opposing players and fans got on him without mercy and without letup. They called Jackie 'shoe-shine boy' and a 'nigger' and a 'black S.O.B.,' and they filled in the initials. They hollered at him that he wasn't good enough to play major league baseball and that the only reason he was on the Dodgers was to attract black fans to Ebbets Field.

It was a vicious and explosive situation. Jackie was our first baseman in his rookie season, and he had to tag that bag faster than any other first baseman in history because if he didn't, he'd get his foot cut off.

Jackie made us better because of his ability and he made us closer because of his suffering. The Dodgers helped to make him a major-leaguer, and he helped to make us champions."

Dodgers great Duke Snider was Robinson's teammate and friend. He admired Jackie's courage in the face of racism.

In his first game with Montreal, Robinson's amazing ballplaying terrorized the opposing team. His team won 14–1.

playing before a large crowd that included many curious Brooklyn fans from across the Hudson River, were terrorized by the Royals' new addition: Robinson hit three singles and a three-run home run and stole two bases. Montreal trounced the Giants fourteen to one.

Incidents of Racism

In Robinson's preparatory season with the Dodgers' top farm club in Montreal, he would prove to the Dodgers' management that he was an excellent ballplayer. He would also show that he could keep his composure in the face of racism on and off the field.

In Baltimore Jackie was injured during a play at second base. The runner came in sliding, and Jackie, covering the base, refused to jump back and away from the upraised spikes on the runner's shoes, which were aimed for Robinson's legs. Jackie was cut badly; the runner was safe at second. Though bleeding and in obvious pain, Jackie demanded to stay in the game. Later in the inning the runner slid home, and Dodgers catcher Herman Franks tagged him hard on the head, in revenge for what had happened to his teammate. There was a scene—a fistfight almost erupted—but the umpires intervened. The Baltimore fans, though, were very agitated. Abuse rained down on the Royals from the stands and racial slurs were aimed at the black second baseman.

Baseball fans in Montreal that season saw the prejudice Robinson withstood, and they cheered liberally for him. The community tried to make Robinson and Rachel, whom he married in February 1946, feel at

handle all the pressure and taunts from bigoted fans and ballplayers. And the treatment he would receive would be enough to unnerve anyone.

The press would be testing him, too; every bat of an eyelash or disapproving frown from him could be translated by reporters into some important statement on race relations. He would not have the luxury of simply playing good baseball.

The most important factor in his success would be the ability to keep his composure. A man without it would surely cause baseball's "great experiment" to fail. An angry, violent black man would cause whites to fear integration. In 1947 it was up to Jackie Robinson to prove how much one individual of indomitable spirit could help to change a whole society.

On opening day with the Montreal Royals, Jackie Robinson showed the world that Branch Rickey had made the right choice. The home-team Jersey City Giants, home. One sportswriter later commented, "For Jackie Robinson and the city of Montreal, it was love at first sight." He was right. After the rejections, unpleasantness, and uncertainties, it was encouraging to find an atmosphere of complete acceptance and something approaching adulation. One of the reasons for the reception the Robinsons received in Montreal was that people there were proud of the team that bore their city's name. As Jackie recalls:

> The people of Montreal were warm and wonderful to us. We rented a pretty apartment in the French-Canadian sector. Our neighbors and everyone we encountered were so attentive and kind to us that we had very little privacy. We were stared at on the street, but the stares were friendly. Kids trailed along behind us, an adoring retinue.[48]

By the end of the season Robinson had won the league batting title. He had led his team to the pennant and the International League's Little World Series. He was considered by many to be a perfect gentleman and humble ballplayer. Also, in November 1946, Jackie Robinson Jr., was born. All in all, it had been a successful year in Montreal for Jackie Robinson.

Cuba

In the spring of 1947 Robinson joined the Royals and Dodgers in sunny Havana, Cuba, where the two teams were getting in shape for the 1947 season. Branch Rickey had chosen Havana over the Dodgers' traditional spring training site in Florida to avoid the Southern segregation laws. He

Jackie, Jackie Jr., and Rachel in 1947. Robinson's first year with Montreal brought him fame on the field and a new son at home.

also wanted to take advantage of Cuba's reputation as an international city that had no prejudice against people of color. Rickey hoped that the liberal atmosphere of Cuba would help smooth Robinson's transition with the Dodgers players.

But the situation was anything but smooth. While the rest of the Royals and Dodgers were put up at the elegant Nacional Hotel in downtown Havana, Robinson and two new blacks on the Royals team, Don Newcombe and Roy Partlow, found themselves housed in a musty hotel fifteen miles from the practice fields.

Robinson protested the arrangement. He told the Dodgers' traveling secretary, who was in charge of hotel accommodations, "I thought we left Florida to train in Cuba so we could get away from Jim Crow [discrimination]. . . . So what the devil is this business of segregating the Negro players in a colored nation, Cuba?"[49] To Cuban authorities, he stated that he thought this kind of segregation was endured only in the United States. He learned that "living arrangements had not been made by local authorities but by Mr. Rickey. [Robinson] was told that [Rickey] felt his plans for [the black ballplayers] were on the threshold of success and he didn't want a possible racial incident to jeopardize his program. [Robinson] reluctantly accepted the explanation."[50] He was later informed that Rickey made the arrangements specifically to quiet some of the Dodgers players who were furious about the possibility of sleeping in the same hotel as a black man.

As spring training came to a close and it became clear that Robinson would be called up to play with the Dodgers, some of the other Dodgers players—Hugh Casey, Bobby Bragan, Dixie Walker, and Carl Furillo—tried to block these plans. They did not want a black player on the team. Petitions were passed around.

One of the players got drunk one night and let it slip to a Dodgers aide that there was a plot to keep Robinson off the Dodgers, and Rickey learned of the story. Infuriated, he called all the suspected ringleaders into his office. He made it clear that anyone signing a petition would leave the club; they weren't needed or wanted. One of the players, reserve catcher Bobby Bragan, still refused to play on the same team with Robinson.

Rickey was adamant in his beliefs. As Robinson would later recall, Rickey

> put down the rebellion with steamroller effectiveness. [Rickey] said later, "I have always believed that a little show of force at the right time is necessary when there's a deliberate violation of law. . . . I believe that when a man is

Robinson waves to fans before disappearing into the clubhouse. The Montreal fans quickly accepted him.

A Teammate from Alabama

Born in Alabama, Dixie Walker was a teammate of Robinson's. There was much written in the newspapers of the subtle friction between the white Southerner and the only black man in baseball. Dixie Walker's brother Harry, a former player himself, tried to explain the attitudes of people from his part of the country, and went on to acknowledge Robinson's abilities in Maury Allen's biography of Robinson:

"I know there was a lot written then about Dixie and Jackie, and I think you have to understand the times. We didn't have much contact with black folks, and when Dixie said what he did it was like a man seeing a green door and not wanting to open it because you didn't know what was behind it. I think we just didn't know what it would be like when the blacks came into baseball.

After a while we all got to playing with the colored players, and there was no fuss made about it. The Cardinals and the Dodgers had a great rivalry and so did the Phillies and the Dodgers when I went over there. Jackie was a great player, and you had to be real alert to play against him. He had catlike ability, and he could accelerate so fast. He never shut that motor down.

Jackie was always fired up in a game. It was great to play against him because he made you play your best. What was interesting from the standpoint of drawing fans was that Jackie drew fans all over the league in those days, but the other colored players didn't. Even when Willie Mays came into the league in 1951, he never drew fans the way Jackie did. Willie wasn't as hungry as Jackie was. He didn't play with that same fire day in and day out."

Alabama-born Dodgers outfielder Dixie Walker had difficulty accepting Robinson's presence on the team.

In his first game as a Dodger, Robinson played first base. Here, he fields the pitcher's attempt to pick off the base runner.

involved in an overt act of violence or in destruction of someone's rights, that it's no time to conduct an experiment in education or persuasion." [Rickey] said he would carry out his plan, regardless of protest. Anyone who was not willing to have a black teammate could quit. The petition protest collapsed before it got started.[51]

Bragan was sent down to the minor leagues.

Shortly afterwards, a group of players on the St. Louis Cardinals were so upset with rumors that a black man was about to be called up to major league baseball that they tried to put together a league-wide strike. League president Ford Frick responded by issuing a warning that anyone taking part in the strike would be kicked out of baseball, even if it meant half the league would be dismissed and the game ruined for years. "This is the United States of America," the baseball president asserted, "and one citizen has as much right to play as another."[52]

The Beginning of Segregation's End

The rumors of a black man in major league baseball came true on the morning of April 9, 1947, near the end of spring training. On that morning, just before an exhibition game, reporters covering the game received a one-page press release with a small announcement at the top: "Brooklyn announces the purchase of the contract of Jack Roosevelt Robinson from Montreal. Signed, Branch Rickey."

Less than a week later, on April 15, 1947—opening day—Jackie Robinson emerged from the Brooklyn Dodgers dugout and trotted across the field to take his defensive position at first base. But his debut as first baseman for the Dodgers was not all that spectacular. Robinson later recalled:

I did a miserable job. There was an overflow crowd at Ebbets Field. If they expected any miracles out of Robinson, they were sadly disappointed. I was in another slump. I grounded out to the third baseman, flied out to left field, bounced into a double play, was safe on an error, and, later, was removed as a defensive safeguard. . . . [There were those who] doubted that I could field and some who hoped I would flunk out and thus establish that blacks weren't ready for the majors.[53]

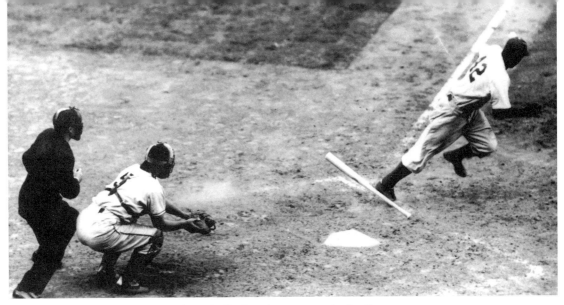

Jackie bunts safely in a game against the Dodgers' crosstown rivals, the Giants. Though he did not play well in his first few games, Robinson was a huge draw at the box office and an instant hero to many blacks.

Although he repeated the dismal performance in his second game, in his third game he smashed a home run against the New York Giants. In his fourth game, more than fifty-two thousand fans crowded into the stadium to see Robinson hit safely and get on base in three out of his four times at bat.

For several weeks after his performance against the Giants, however, Robinson went in and out of a slump. His hitting was poor. He felt uncomfortable in the infield and was charged with several errors. There were opportunities for him to be a hero, but time after time he failed to rise to the occasion. His teammates generally avoided him. No one came to talk to him in the locker room. And on the field, when he broke from his slump to hit a home run, no one was waiting at home plate to shake his hand or slap him on the back. His teammates treated him as they would any other rookie. They were waiting for Robinson to prove himself as a consistent, capable ballplayer.

Even though Robinson played poorly, his mere presence profoundly affected attendance at the stadiums. In support of Robinson, black fans began filling stadiums everywhere he played. In 1947, the season of Robinson's debut, attendance in the National League rose by 750,000 people more than the previous record-setting year, 1946. Attendance at the Dodgers games skyrocketed to 1.8 million. Bill Russell, the basketball star, would later declare that the Dodgers "picked up 20 million fans instantly."[54]

Many of these black fans were children. Whether they lived in Brooklyn, Atlanta, Texas, or California, virtually all black children cheered the newest Brooklyn Dodger. Baseball superstar Hank Aaron, a student at a segregated high school in Mobile, Alabama, at the time of the Robinson signing, recalled that "every black kid in Mobile, every black kid who played baseball in this country, became Dodger fans."[55]

Robinson Faces Adversity

From the beginning Robinson was exposed to the hatred of bigots. Hate mail arrived in the Dodgers clubhouse every day. While other players got adoring cards and letters from young fans, requesting autographs or responses, Robinson received warnings to get out of town. His life and family were threatened. All he could do was try to ignore this outpouring of hatred.

From the stands abuse rained down on Robinson every time he stepped out of the dugout. If a pitch was called in his favor, fans would first violently berate the umpire with cries of "Nigger lover!" then continue their taunting of Robinson. Everywhere he turned an angry voice yelled something intended to hurt and offend.

It was often hard for other players to watch Robinson restraining himself. Joe Black was Robinson's teammate on the Dodgers and remembered one incident.

> I remember one time we walked on the field and some loudmouth started yelling at him from the stands. "Hey, Jackie, king of the niggers, hey Jackie."

Then he began singing "Old Black Joe" and calling Jackie a coon and screaming all kinds of vile things at him.

> Jackie just stared straight ahead, but you knew he was burning inside. He was a combative person by nature and that restraint went against his personality. He had to hold a lot in, and it angered him terribly. Holding that much anger can really hurt a man, and I think all that name calling in those years killed him. I really do think that.[56]

Bench jockeys—players on opposing teams who shouted insults from the safety of their dugout—were relentless. Robinson nearly blew the whole experiment when confronted by one of the most notorious of the bench jockeys, Ben ("Monk") Chapman, the manager of the Philadelphia Phillies. Chapman, a Southerner, had been brought up in a racist and anti-Semitic environment, and his attitudes toward blacks and Jews were extreme. In fact, he had even been known to hurl anti-Semitic remarks at fans in the stadiums.

When the Phillies played the Dodgers for the first time that season, Robinson was met with abuse from Chapman's dugout

Philadelphia Phillies manager Ben Chapman greets Robinson before the rookie's first game against the Phillies in May 1947. Chapman led the Phillies' verbal abuse of Robinson and nearly destroyed the young player's composure.

Robinson's Detractors

Ben Chapman was a notorious bench jockey. In an interview for Maury Allen's biography of Robinson, Chapman describes the tactics he used on Robinson:

"I didn't like the idea he was pushed in the game. There were other players more qualified to be in the big leagues that year. Rickey wanted Robinson. That wasn't right. He should have been made to earn his chance.

Sure, we rode him. We rode everybody. They rode Babe Ruth and Lou Gehrig when I went to the Yankees. Everybody in baseball understood that was part of the game. We knocked him down. We knocked everybody down. I didn't tell my Phillies ball club to ride him more than anybody else. I just told them to treat him like they would treat any other rookie. We got on every new player to see if he could take it.

I'd been around colored people before I saw Robinson. We saw colored people in Birmingham. They had their schools and things, and they would come downtown to shop and nobody thought anything of it. I think a lot of what happened was caused by the newspapers up there looking for a scapegoat for Robinson. I wound up as the bad guy, and they wrote a lot of things about me that caused me a lot of trouble. I don't want to go into detail now because it's so many years ago. Look, I had a good career and played fifteen years and even came back during the war to pitch in Brooklyn. I had a lifetime average of .302 and played on one of the greatest teams of all times, the 1932 Yankees, and I never get mentioned for the Hall of Fame. Do you know why that is? I think it is because of all the bad publicity I got involving all that business. I think Jackie Robinson kept me out of the Hall of Fame.

I got to admire the boy after I saw him play a few times. He was one of the best competitors I ever saw. He could beat you more ways than you could curry a mule."

that shocked him: "Starting to the plate in the first inning, I could scarcely believe my ears. Almost as if it had been synchronized by some master conductor, hate poured forth from the Phillies dugout:

Hey, nigger, why don't you go back to the cotton field where you belong?

They're waiting for you in the jungles, black boy!

Hey, snowflake, which one of those white boys' wives are you dating tonight?

We don't want you here, nigger.

Go back to the bushes!"

Robinson later recalled that "those insults and taunts were only samples of the torrent of abuse which poured out from the Phillies dugout that April day."[57] Robinson, enraged, nearly lost his temper.

For one wild and rage-crazed minute I thought, "To hell with Mr. Rickey's 'noble experiment.' It's clear it won't succeed. . . ." I thought what a glorious, cleansing thing it would be to let go. To hell with the image of the patient black freak I was supposed to create. I could throw down my bat, stride over to that Phillies dugout, grab one of those white sons of bitches and smash his teeth in with my despised black fist.[58]

But Robinson was able to control himself. He thought about all the hard work and faith Rickey and his family had put into this effort to break baseball's color barrier. And he thought of his son's saying to his own children, some day way in the future, that Jackie Robinson Sr., could have been a star if he hadn't been too much of a man. "Then, I thought of Mr. Rickey—how his family and friends had begged him not to fight for me and my people. I thought of all his predictions, which had come true. Mr. Rickey had come to a crossroads and made a lonely decision. I was at a crossroads. I would make mine. I would stay."[59]

Years later Robinson would declare that the Phillies had beaten him on that day. The constant insults had shaken him up and made him play badly. The torrent of abuse continued during the next two games between the teams. By the third game Robinson's teammates had had enough. Eddie Stanky got up and roared to the Phillies bench, "You bunch of yellow-bellied cowards! Why don't you pick on someone who could yell back?"

Other Dodgers rose and yelled curses and challenges across the field. Robinson remembered what Rickey had said: that if the Dodgers respected him, they would stand up for him. Much to Robinson's relief and pleasure, Rickey had been right.

Teammate Eddie Stanky was the first to defend Robinson against the onslaught of abuse he endured from opposing players.

After the incident in Philadelphia, attitudes among Robinson's teammates changed. They knew that under Rickey's instructions Jackie could not yell back, and they began to stick up for him. Al Campanis, an infielder with the Dodgers, "used to let them yell a little, and then [he] would yell back. 'You wanna pick on somebody, pick on me.' They would yell, 'We don't have anything against you.' It was all ridiculous."[60]

Author Joseph Nazel explains the lesson learned by the Dodgers in the face of Robinson's torment and points out that the lesson had a positive aspect, too:

> The incident with the Phillies had at least one major result which was a step forward in race relations. It brought the Dodgers together in defense of Jackie Robinson. At that moment they realized that Jackie was part of *their* team. He was a part of the whole. What happened to Jackie happened to them. They had learned something that Jackie had practiced throughout his sports career, the importance of team loyalty. The team comes first! Of course the negative aspect of the Dodgers' sudden show of unity was that many were only protecting *their* "Negro" because he *belonged* to them. The unity did not involve *equality*.[61]

Robinson was not immune to the pressures of racism. One night, distraught over the perpetual insults and threats, Robinson called his sister Willa Mae in Pasadena. She knew from the tone of his voice that he was deeply disturbed. He wanted to quit and come home. Willa Mae, Mack, and their mother all did their best to console him and give him courage: "I could tell just how bad he felt," recalled Willa Mae. "He was fed up fighting it every day of his life then."[62]

Breaking Out of a Slump

With the support of his family and teammates, Robinson, always the proud and fearless competitor, began playing up to his potential. He was successful at bat and ran aggressively on the base paths. He was more sure of himself at first base. His teammates began to praise and support him.

In several games, when the Dodgers were losing, Robinson was able to turn the course of a game around. Robinson would

Jackie was a daring base runner. He gets caught here in a rundown between the Cubs' catcher and third baseman.

combine his skills in the field and as a batter with gutsy and unnerving tactics as a base runner. Once on base, either by a walk or a line drive single to the outfield, Robinson began his game. He played a kind of cat and mouse game with the pitcher. Robinson would take a few steps toward second base, daring the pitcher to make him return to first base, and the pitcher, unnerved by this moving threat, would indeed throw to first, to keep Robinson there. This strategy of movement and threat, repeated continuously, shifted the concentration of the pitcher from the batter, where it was supposed to be, to Robinson. This maneuver was always to the batter's advantage: a distracted pitcher was likely to pitch badly.

Whether or not the batter could take advantage of the distraction that had been created, Robinson would find a way to score a run. Roger Kahn describes in loving prose the beauty of Robinson on the base paths:

> Breaking, Robinson reached full speed in three strides. The pigeon-toed walk yielded to a run of graceful power. He could steal home, or advance two bases on someone else's bunt, and at the time of decision, when he slid, the big dark body became a bird in flight. Then, safe, he rose slowly, often limping, and made his pigeon-toed way to the dugout.[63]

The Dodgers united as a team and ended the season strongly. They won the National League pennant and went to the 1947 World Series to face the American League champions, the New York Yankees.

Robinson regarded opening day of the World Series as one of the most important moments in his life. "It was a history-mak-

Jackie slides into third. His quickness often enabled him to reach third from first on the next batter's single.

ing day. It would be the first time that a black man would be allowed to participate in a World Series. I had become the first black player in the major leagues."[64]

The Dodgers struggled to win the Series but were unable to clinch it. Robinson played effectively but was less than spectacular. He was magnificent on the base paths, unnerving the opposing New York Yankees pitchers, and he batted and fielded well—but the Yankees were just too strong. The Dodgers lost the Series to the Yankees in seven hard-fought games.

In a time-honored tradition, shortly after the conclusion of each World Series the *Sporting News,* one of the sports world's oldest and most revered publications, selects baseball's Rookie of the Year. Traditionally the award goes to a gifted player fresh out of high school or college. At the close of the 1947 season Jackie Robinson was named Rookie of the Year. Robinson was already twenty-eight years old and no newcomer to baseball.

The fact that he was chosen as Rookie of the Year points to his tremendous ability as a ballplayer and not the fact that he was black. According to the *Sporting News,* Robinson

> might have had more obstacles than his first year competitors, and that he perhaps had a harder fight to gain even major league recognition, was no concern of this publication. The sociological experiment that Robinson represented, the trail-blazing that he did, the barriers he broke down, did not enter into the decision. He was rated and examined solely as a freshman player in the big leagues on the basis of his hitting, his running, his defensive play, his team value.[65]

Robinson had proven, by the end of his first season with the Dodgers, that he was more than just a black man in baseball: he was an exceptional player who deserved to compete with the best players in America. Ability, not skin color, was the supreme factor in determining excellence. This message, vital to the integration of baseball, was vital, too, to the forces of integration at work throughout American society. With Jackie Robinson's appearance in baseball,

> an era of racial exclusiveness in sports died. Racism did not die with dignity and grace, and, indeed, its pale ghost still hovers about the front offices, the coaches' boxes, and the managers' lockers of professional baseball. But the overt phenomenon [of racism] is

Robinson is tagged out trying to score on an overthrow. In part because of his exciting style, Jackie was named Rookie of the Year in 1947.

Robinson is congratulated after hitting a home run in one of his first games as a Dodger. Robinson proved many times that a black ballplayer was just as effective as a white one.

dead; and the speed, the skill, and the dignity of Jackie Robinson did more to lay it to rest than those of any other single individual. Before Robinson gave it the lie for all time, the legend was that blacks and whites would never play together as a team. Individual blacks might run track (Jesse Owens), or excel in the ring (Joe Louis), or perform any number of feats by themselves, but they could never command the respect that would make white athletes want to play with them. That is all history now.[66]

Quote

4 Robinson Unleashed

Baseball's color barrier, on the whole, had fallen. Blacks had begun entering organized baseball on the heels of Jackie Robinson. Larry Doby was signed in the summer of 1947 to the Cleveland Indians and became the first black player in the American League. By the spring of 1948 Roy Campanella had been signed by Branch Rickey to play with the Brooklyn Dodgers and Don Newcombe, who was playing in the minor leagues, would join in 1949. Monte Irvin was signed by the New York Giants in 1948 and played for them the following year. By 1948 blacks were making steady progress integrating organized baseball. Some Americans, however, were trying to keep the color barrier in place.

The Ku Klux Klan had been founded in 1866, right after the Civil War. The aim of this secret organization was to conduct a campaign of terror against newly freed blacks, whom the Klan, dressed in hooded white sheets, threatened, beat, and lynched. The Klan was disbanded in 1869 but formed again in 1915 and included among its targets Jews, Catholics, and the foreign born. In the Ku Klux Creed, which is the Klan's statement of belief, one of the passages acknowledges that they will be "true in the faithful maintenance of White Supremacy and will strenuously oppose any compromise thereof in any and all things."[67]

As spring training began for the 1949 season, the Ku Klux Klan made a very serious threat. Through reports in the Atlanta newspapers, the grand dragon of the Klan warned the Dodgers that Robinson and Campanella would not be allowed to play an exhibition game in Atlanta. The Klan leader insisted that there were state laws prohibiting interracial games. When legal officials found no such laws, the grand

Future Hall of Famer Roy Campanella signed with the Dodgers in 1948.

A year after Robinson joined the Dodgers, Monte Irvin became the first black player signed by the New York Giants.

dragon claimed that if the Dodgers came to Atlanta with black ballplayers there would be bloody violence.

Knowing full well the potential for violence, Robinson refused to be deterred by the Klan's threats. He had a serious talk with Campanella, urging him to take the field, not to back down. Campanella agreed. The two men discussed the matter with Branch Rickey, who gave them his full support. Rickey predicted that nothing would come of the threats.

Rickey was right. Almost fifty thousand fans turned out for the Dodgers' three games against the Atlanta Crackers, and a large number of those fans were black. In the final Sunday game, nearly fourteen thousand blacks came to the ball park.

They filled up the segregated section in the outfield bleachers. They stood shoulder to shoulder behind the outfield fence. They cheered on the visiting Dodgers. There were no incidents.

Though hate groups like the Klan would continue to protest the integration of baseball, for the most part fans in Atlanta and throughout the South supported integration, but they especially supported Robinson. He had filled them with pride and gave them newfound hope and confidence in the future.

After the series in Atlanta was over, Robinson declared his appreciation for being put in the position to help build this feeling of confidence: "I wouldn't trade shoes with any man in the world."[68] *Quote*

White-robed Ku Klux Klan members burn a cross as part of a white supremacist ceremony. The Klan opposed the desegregation of baseball.

A New Robinson

With the outpouring of support and the absence of violence, Robinson believed Branch Rickey's censorship of his conduct should end. He felt he had earned the right to be treated as any other ballplayer. He and Rickey talked this over, and Rickey agreed that Robinson had earned the right to act with less restraint than he had displayed the prior two seasons. Recalled Rickey:

> I realized the point would come when my almost filial relationship with Jackie would break with ill feeling if I did not issue an emancipation proclamation for him. I could see how the tensions had built up in two years and that this young man had come through with courage far beyond what I asked, yet, I knew that burning inside him was the same pride and determination that burned inside those Negro slaves a century earlier. I knew also that while the wisest policy for Robinson during those first two years was to turn the other cheek and not fight back, there were many in baseball who would not understand his lack of action. They could be made to respect only the fighting back, the things that are the signs of courage to men who know courage only in its physical sense. So I told Robinson that he was on his own. Then I sat back happily, knowing that, with the restraints removed, Robinson was going to show the National League a thing or two.[69]

Upon his arrival that spring in Vero Beach, Florida, Robinson made an announcement that drew everyone's attention. He declared in an interview that opposing players "better be prepared to be rough this year, because I'm going to be rough on them." He kept his word. During spring training he nearly came to blows with rookie teammate Chris Van Cuyk. The rookie pitcher had thrown the ball too close to Robinson's head in batting practice. Robinson yelled at Van Cuyk, threats were exchanged, and teammates had to step in to keep the two men from blows. During a game with Philadelphia, Phillies pitcher Schoolboy Rowe and Robinson almost got in a fistfight.

This type of animosity between teams was not unusual. Opposing players threatened each other openly in the press. On the field pitchers threw at batters' heads, and on the base paths men like Ty Cobb

Pitching ace Schoolboy Rowe was aggressively challenged by Robinson after throwing a pitch too close to Robinson's head.

Never Just Another Guy

In Jackie Robinson: First of the Chosen Few, *author and baseball writer Joseph Nazel discusses an important moment in Robinson's second season that caused many baseball commentators to see the black ballplayer as "just another guy":*

"Jackie's one great hope was to be treated like any other ball player. And by that he meant he wanted to be **Jackie Robinson** and all that that meant, and still be accepted on equal terms with the other players. It was a great deal to ask of white America, but Jackie felt that he was finally getting his point across when, in 1948, he was thrown out of a game for heckling an umpire. The newspaper headlines expressed Jackie's hope in large print: **JACKIE JUST ANOTHER GUY!**

The news account glowed with the report that Jackie Robinson was being treated fairly. Baseball had shown a nobility to be praised. Jackie's being thrown out reflected a growth in baseball. He was thrown out because he heckled, not because he was black. And more importantly, the umpire did his duty even though Jackie was black. Jackie was not being treated with kid gloves.

The truth is, Jackie wasn't 'just another guy.' He was a black man in a world conditioned to see him as an inferior, as incapable of major accomplishment, and unworthy of basic human rights and citizenship privileges."

---

almost always slid into base with their spiked shoes aimed at the opposing player's legs. Fistfights were not at all uncommon.

What made these incidents unusual was that Robinson was black. In the United States in 1949 black men did not stand up to white men, and they never initiated an attack. In the eyes of whites, blacks were still considered legitimate targets of violence. In almost any city or town throughout the nation, a black man thought to have looked "the wrong way" at a white man or woman could find himself running for his life from a white mob.

Lynchings, though less common than during the 1920s, were still a serious threat.

Now free to defend himself against individuals who taunted or threatened him, Robinson had a remarkable impact on blacks. Black fans were filled with pride because Robinson would not stand for abuse. Writer Maury Allen contends that "blacks across America were inspired by his success. They began to think in terms of their own success. The first measurable movement began, of course, in baseball. That was the avenue Robinson had used and blacks across America wanted to follow."[70] Robinson later recalled,

(Left to right)
Jackie Robinson, Larry Doby,
Don Newcombe, Luke Easter,
and Roy Campanella pose to-
gether before a 1950 game in
Brooklyn.

I could fight back when I wanted. That sounds as though I wanted to get even, and I'm sure that is partly true. But more than revenge . . . I wanted to be Jackie Robinson, and for the first time I would be justified because by 1949 the principle had been established: the major victory won. There were enough blacks on other teams to ensure that American baseball could never again turn its back on minority competitors.[71]

Helping Other Players

After breaking baseball's color barrier, Robinson did his best to help the black players who followed him into the major leagues. Don Newcombe, who joined the Brooklyn Dodgers in 1949, was the third black man on the team after Robinson and Roy Campanella, who had joined in 1948, and he received much help from Robinson.

Robinson tried to help black players on opposing teams, too. When Willie Mays

came to the New York Giants in 1951, Robinson tried to help him, even though the Giants and Dodgers were arch rivals. He would speak to Mays on the phone at night, explaining what had to be ignored by a black man in baseball and what had to be done, and also how to bat against certain pitchers and what to expect from certain ball clubs. Robinson would never give away any secrets about the Dodgers,

Robinson counseled Giants newcomer Willie Mays during Mays's first major league season.

though! The result of Robinson's efforts was that Mays and other black players around the league did not feel so alone. They would learn to heed his advice and seek his opinions.

Because Robinson always tried to be as candid as possible, the media, too, would seek his opinions. Even when asked uncomfortable questions—about, for example, managers who still race-baited him from opposing dugouts—he obliged the press by speaking the truth as best he could. Of course, not everyone was pleased with his candor.

One day in 1949, while speaking out against certain umpires he often disagreed with, Robinson interjected race into the issue: "I have no doubt that there are some umpires in the National League who are 'on' me."[72] This remark was interpreted by many to mean that there was a conspiracy against him because he was black. The

Robinson challenges an umpire's call after being picked off at second base. Robinson believed that some umpires let racial prejudice cloud their judgment.

Robinson and the Press

Harvey Frommer notes in his book Rickey and Robinson, *that those involved in baseball—especially reporters who covered the games—found Robinson disagreeable, beginning with the 1949 season, and they took him to task for it:*

"Aggressiveness on and off the field made him a mark as the mild-mannered, soft-spoken, self-effacing image was replaced by one that was determined, outspoken, socially conscious. The code words used to describe him were 'hothead,' 'crusader,' 'troublemaker,' 'pop-off.' The hidden definition for these labels was clearly understood by Robinson.

Many times his fights were with the press. Some sportswriters told him that his attitudes would cost him awards. His response was that any trophy won for being a 'good kid' would be of no value to him."

Changing Baseball Forever

In Maury Allen's biography of Robinson, A Life Remembered, Lou Brock, a black Hall of Fame player with the St. Louis Cardinals, describes what it meant to be a Jackie Robinson fan:

"Where I grew up in Collinston, Louisiana, blacks were sharecroppers, dirt farmers, not baseball players. We picked cotton and corn and talked about the reality of our lives.

Then Jackie Robinson came along in 1947. I was eight years old then, and my thoughts about professional baseball were changed forever. Baseball had been a white, society, country-club game. There was no room in it for blacks. Everybody knew that. Then there were pictures of Robinson, that black face, in the newspapers, and it hit us with the impact of an H-bomb. He touched our world. We could have a fantasy, too, just like the white kids; we could dream of playing that great American pastime in huge stadiums before big crowds. It meant more than just baseball to us. It meant we didn't have to be dirt farmers anymore. It meant we could have our dreams and go out and make something of ourselves. We could look at the farm master and tell him we were leaving. We would live our own dreams. We could play baseball in that fantasy world if we wanted, and if we were good enough."

St. Louis Cardinals Hall of Famer Lou Brock was a fan of Jackie Robinson.

comment was met with scorn and out-rage from umpires around the league, and the baseball commissioner protested—but Robinson insisted he was just giving his opinion, that this was his right. As newspaper columnist Dick Young pointed out that year: "Robinson has reached the stage where he says what he believes and says it without reservation, which is a trait unfortunately frowned on in most social circles."[73]

But saying what he strongly believed and felt was an essential characteristic of Jackie Robinson and helped lead to his success. As Jules Tygiel relates, "It was this fury of Robinson that enabled him to do the great and immensely difficult thing that he did."[74]

Robinson's celebrity status affected his teammates in different ways. Some were put off by it. To them, Robinson was being too much of a politician. By readily voicing his opinions, it seemed that he was trying to draw attention to himself as the team leader and spokesman. Monte Irvin, the New York Giants star, insists that some Dodgers would be thinking "don't think for me, [or] tell me what I should do,"[75] while Robinson was being interviewed after a game. Others on the Dodgers, though, appreciated the outspokenness. Many times Robinson said things that they felt but did not want to admit to, like hard feelings toward another team or questions about an umpire's judgment. "Many times

Robinson slides back to first as the opponents' pitcher tries to pick him off. Robinson's aggressive base running distracted the opposing pitcher and improved Jackie's teammates' chances for hits.

when I made strong or controversial statements," Robinson recalled in his autobiography, "I was not fighting for a personal thing. I was standing up for my team. I was saying things some of my teammates felt but were reluctant to say. The Dodgers appreciated this, and it was a refutation of the charge that I was making verbal grandstand plays to promote myself."[76]

In 1949, encouraged by the removal of Branch Rickey's restraints, Robinson's attitude improved and his performance blossomed. On the field Robinson was a terror at bat and on the base paths, and he again led the Dodgers to the National League pennant. He could not lead them to victory in the World Series, though, and the Dodgers fell to the Yankees after a hard-fought, competitive series of games. Nevertheless, Robinson was named baseball's Most Valuable Player.

National League president Ford Frick presents Jackie Robinson with the league's Most Valuable Player award after the 1949 season.

Robinson and Robeson

In 1949 not all the controversy in Jackie Robinson's life revolved around baseball. In July he was asked by the House on Un-American Activities Committee (HUAC) to testify against Paul Robeson.

Born into relative wealth in New Jersey, Robeson had harbored a resentment against the way blacks were treated in America. After attending law school he went into acting, and in 1931 he left America for England. Then he took his son to the Soviet Union (USSR) to become educated. In speaking about the USSR, Robeson insisted that he had found a country where "I walked the earth for the first time with complete dignity."[77]

From his home in Paris in 1949, Robeson commented on the tensions between America and the Soviet Union. He stated that blacks in America would not fight the Soviet Union for America. This statement made him an ideal target of HUAC.

The House on Un-American Activities Committee was created by Congress in 1938 and gained notoriety after World War II as competition between the Soviet Union and America rose and relations deteriorated. The committee focused its activities on hunting for communists and other people sympathetic to the Soviet Union. In the course of its duties the committee ruined people's careers—including many from show business—using flimsy and unsubstantiated evidence to accuse them of communist sympathies.

Jackie Robinson was invited by the committee to testify that blacks would indeed fight for their country against any aggressor—especially a communist one. At first he was pleased to have been asked by

We Don't Need Communism's Help

In his autobiography, Jackie Robinson recalls his testimony before the House Committee on Un-American Activities:

"I told the committee that I didn't pretend to be an expert on Communism or any other political 'ism,' but I was an expert on being a colored American, having had thirty years of experience at it, and I knew how difficult it was to be in the minority. I felt that we had made some progress in baseball and that we could make progress in other American fields provided we got rid of some of the misunderstandings the public still suffered from. There had been a lot of misunderstanding on the subject of Communism among Negroes in this country that was bound to hurt my people's cause unless it was cleared up. Every Negro worth his salt hated racial discrimination, and if it happened that it was a Communist who denounced discrimination, that didn't change the truth of his charges. It might be true that Communists kicked up a big fuss over racial discrimination because it suited their purposes. However that was no reason to pretend that the whole issue was a creation of the Communist imagination. . . .

I am a religious man. Therefore I cherish America where I am free to worship as I please, a privilege which some countries do not give. And I suspect that nine hundred and ninety-nine out of almost any thousand colored Americans you meet will tell you the same thing.

But that doesn't mean that we're going to stop fighting race discrimination in this country until we've got it licked. It means that we're going to fight it all the harder because our stake in the future is so big. We can win our fight without the Communists and we don't want their help."

Jackie testifies before Congress.

the committee to come to Washington. He interpreted the invitation as a sign that his appeal was nationwide and that his opinion was of value to people in high places.

But Robinson was in conflict, too. He knew that by opposing Robeson and arguing that the United States was not a bad place for blacks, he would be expressing an opinion unpopular in much of the black community. He did not want to be seen as being used by whites to pit blacks against each other. Yet he did not side with what Robeson said—he thought Robeson was making too much of an assumption by saying that all blacks would not fight. Robinson was not one to let another man speak for him. Jackie talked with Rachel for many long, difficult hours. Finally he decided to accept the invitation to Washington.

In his speech before HUAC on July 18, 1949, Robinson gave an eloquent, carefully worded defense of black civil rights. He condemned Robeson and the communists and even took a jab at Robeson by referring to the man's rich singing voice: "I've got too much invested for my wife and child and myself in the future of this country . . . to throw it away because of a siren song sung in bass."[78]

By speaking his mind with clarity and eloquence on a difficult subject, Robinson had made himself an example of free-thinking for American blacks. Many, however, viewed him with disappointment. The author Martin Duberman reports that one prominent black columnist, J. A. Rogers, "expressed agreement with many of Robinson's sentiments but disapproved of the auspices under which he had delivered them." A black newspaper ran a cartoon "depicting a frightened little boy labeled Jackie Robinson with a huge gun

Jackie and Rachel leave the Capitol after he testified to Congress that black Americans were loyal to the United States.

in his hand, uncertainly tracking the giant footprints of Paul Robeson."[79]

Years later Robinson would come to rethink his participation in the proceeding, recognizing the hardships Robeson suffered in speaking out against injustice, and admitting that whites had not been especially efficient about seeking justice.

That statement was made over twenty years ago, and I have never regretted it. But I have grown wiser and closer to painful truths about America's destructiveness. And I do have an increased respect for Paul Robeson who, over the span of that twenty years, sacrificed himself, his career, and the wealth and comfort he once enjoyed because, I believe, he was sincerely trying to help his people."[80]

Robinson on the Big Screen

In baseball's off-season Robinson received a call from Hollywood: Would he agree to star in a film about his life? The studio, Eagle-Lion, wanted to make the movie for several reasons. Robinson's struggle over civil rights made a wonderfully dramatic story about one man's lonely fight for justice. Also, Hollywood businessmen saw the way Robinson had filled baseball stadiums with black people and were sure he would do the same in movie theaters across the nation.

The movie industry in Hollywood at this time was not progressive in its attitudes toward blacks. Black actors played the parts of clowns or servants. A black man or woman in film had never been portrayed as an individual, and the effects of prejudice on blacks had never been dramatized. By making a film about Robinson, Eagle-Lion would be breaking new ground.

After hearing the producers' offer, Robinson conferred with Rickey. The two men came up with some requirements. First, they wanted the movie to detail the prejudice Robinson had experienced. Second, they insisted on the hiring of as many black ballplayers for the film as possible. Both demands were met by the film's producers.

The film *The Jackie Robinson Story* was made in three weeks. The producers wanted to complete it before spring training for the 1950 baseball season, and the crew and cast worked day and night. Robinson later "realized it had been made too quickly, that it was budgeted

Robinson played himself in the 1950 film of his life story.

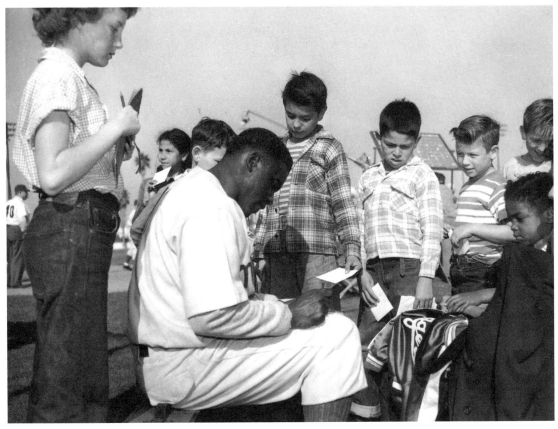

Jackie, now a film star as well as a baseball star, signs autographs on the movie set during a break in shooting.

too low, and that, if it had been made later in [his] career, it could have been done much better."[81]

The film received mixed reviews. While there were many fine scenes taken directly from Robinson's life, critics felt that some incidents were corny. Robinson's acting, though, got rave reviews. Through all the scenes, as one reviewer put it, "the magnificent athlete conducts himself with dignity, speaks his lines well and clearly and faces the camera squarely, with neither shyness nor conceit. Acting, they say, is largely timing—it is movement coordinated naturally. That is in Jackie Robinson's department."[82]

In spite of what the critics said, Americans welcomed the chance to watch the baseball hero closeup, on the big screen. In darkened theaters, adults saw a black's life depicted in a way never seen before. Youngsters sat with their eyes fixed on the black hero suffering the indignities of racism yet rising, each time, to conquer his fears. A generation of Americans witnessed the moving story of a man overcoming the barriers imposed on him because of the color of his skin.

5 A Tireless Crusader

In the early fifties integration continued its advance on segregated America. By 1950 the armed forces had abolished segregation in any form. In education, color barriers began to break: the state of Texas, forced by the United States Supreme Court to create equal conditions for black and white law students, opened the doors of its University of Texas Law School to blacks. In sports, Nat ("Sweetwater") Clifton, formerly

John Saunders Chase, the first black admitted to the University of Texas, waits in line to register for law school in 1950.

a star with the all-black Harlem Globetrotters, became the first professional black basketball player with the New York Knicks in 1950.

But progress was not complete, and blacks continued to fear violence at the hands of whites. Black veterans of World War II were bombed out of houses they had purchased in white neighborhoods throughout America. In Albany, Georgia, sharecropper Rosa Lee Ingram and her sons, Sammie, fourteen, and Wallace, sixteen, had all recently been sentenced to death for killing, in self-defense, an armed white farmer who had attacked them as the family worked in the fields. In other parts of the country members of the NAACP were harassed, threatened, and even blown from their beds by bombs planted by white extremist groups like the White Citizens' Council.

Throughout his career with the Dodgers Robinson lived in a climate of violence and fear. Red Barber, the Dodgers radio announcer, once remarked that the air of violence surrounding Jackie Robinson "was not something you were suddenly confronted with one day and then didn't have to worry about anymore. It had to be handled inning by inning, game by game, month by month. It was there all the time, because when Robinson came, he came to stay."[83]

At the beginning of the 1950 season, threatening letters were sent to the Dodgers, the Cincinnati Reds, and Cincinnati's police headquarters and daily newspaper. The letters stated that Robinson would be shot if he entered Crosley Field, home of the Reds. The letters said that a gunman would be positioned in a nearby building.

Cincinnati was an especially hellish place for Robinson to play. As Jules Tygiel points out, "Crosley Field . . . attracted crowds from the racially charged border states of Kentucky and West Virginia, and most facilities in Cincinnati remained segregated into the late 1950s."

"The worst fans were in Cincinnati," recalled [black ballplayer] Hank Thompson. "Whenever there was a lull, some loudmouth would yell: 'Nigger' or 'black unprintable' and you could hear it all over the place."[84]

After learning of the threat, Robinson was frightened but undaunted. Massive security was on hand for the day of the game. FBI agents surrounded the stadium and infiltrated the neighborhood as well as the stands, looking for suspicious individuals. Thousands of blacks were in the stands that day. Many had come a long way from the South to see Robinson and the other blacks on the team play. The FBI was concerned that if there were an assassination attempt there might be additional widespread violence.

As it turned out, no bullets were fired. Robinson and his teammates nervously joked their way through the doubleheader, and Robinson, in fact, hit a home run to win the first of the two games.

This was not the end of threats in Cincinnati, though. In 1952 another death threat would be issued against Robinson,

Nat "Sweetwater" Clifton, signed by the New York Knicks in 1950, was the first black in the National Basketball Association.

who arrived and left Crosley Field accompanied by armed security guards. Cincinnati was not the only origin of these terrifying letters: In 1953, Robinson received a letter from St. Louis stating "You die, no use crying for the cops. You'll be executed gangland style in Busch Stadium."[85] Nothing came of that threat, either—the tenth such threat Robinson had received since agreeing to be part of Branch Rickey's great experiment.

Speaking His Mind

Despite this climate of fear, Robinson was not deterred from speaking his mind as an outspoken advocate for civil rights. Articulate

Like Traveling Through South Africa

Monte Irvin was one of the first black players after Robinson to be signed by a major league team. He played with the New York Giants after an illustrious career in the Negro leagues, where he met Robinson. In Maury Allen's biography of Robinson Irvin recalls that life for the black ballplayers in the Negro leagues could be terrible, but sometimes life for blacks in the majors could be worse:

"Black players today don't understand what Jackie and the rest of us went through in those early days. It's pretty easy for these guys now. I remember going into Philadelphia and getting called every racial name under the sun. The hatred was as plain as the nose on your face. It was like a black traveling in the white part of South Africa these days. We all took a lot to play in the big leagues. Jackie the most of course because he was the first. Nobody, black or white, should ever forget what Jackie did."

Monte Irvin, like Robinson and other black players, coped with bigotry in major league baseball.

and aggressive, unable by nature to conceal what he truly felt, he was given to expressing his own opinions—no matter that they were often controversial. Newspaper stories featured his blunt answers to questions about racism and discrimination.

Robinson had the kind of personality that reporters appreciated. Jules Tygiel offers an explanation for Robinson's popularity among the news media:

> Far more articulate, intelligent, and outspoken than the average person, Robinson represented "good copy" to the press. He answered questions honestly, forthrightly, and with a measure of naivete. "He has the tact of a child, because he has the moral purity of a child," explained [sportswriter] Dick Young. Robinson repeatedly pledged, "That's the last time I'm opening my mouth," but his silence always proved short-lived. Within days, an incident would trigger a long tirade, which Robinson would punctuate with a resounding, "You're damn right you can quote me." Unlike other ballplayers, he never avoided adverse repercussions by denying a controversial statement. "It was almost ridiculous the way reporters made for Robinson's cubicle after the critical games," noted sportswriter John Hanlon. "Others may have starred, but Robinson, all knew, was the one who talked."[86]

Swinging the Heavy Bat

Even in apparently innocuous settings, Robinson would be the one who talked—especially when confronted with questions about discrimination. On November 30, 1952, during an unrehearsed question-and-answer segment on the popular television talk show "Youth Wants To Know," he was asked by a girl in the studio audience if he thought that the New York Yankees had been practicing racial discrimination.

While other teams were integrating, the Yankees had not yet fielded a black ballplayer. According to several reporters, when executives in the Yankee organization were asked about integrating the team, they answered in foul language and used ethnic slurs. It was apparent that the club had an unwritten policy barring blacks from joining the team. And this policy came under pressure in New York, where the three other big-league teams were integrated, and where there was a very large black population.

Now, on national television, Robinson was asked what he thought. Most ballplayers would find a way to duck the question. Who wanted to go on record accusing a team of discrimination when there wasn't any hard proof of it? But Robinson could not keep quiet when he thought he saw injustice. After pausing to think, he responded: "I think the Yankee management is prejudiced. There isn't a single Negro on the team now and very few in the entire Yankee farm system."[87]

As Robinson remembers in his autobiography, the outpouring of anger from all over the country the next day was extraordinary.

> I had no idea—and I am sure that girl never dreamed—that her innocent question and my candid reply would cause all hell to break loose. The next day headline stories were published. A Cleveland writer tried to take me apart

Baseball commissioner Ford Frick supported Jackie's outspoken attitude toward racial injustice.

in an article in which he described me as a "soap box orator" and a "rabble rouser." Many hate letters, a lot of them anonymous, came into our club attacking me.[88]

The Yankees themselves immediately responded to Robinson's comments, saying they had not found a black player good enough for their team, but Robinson refused to retract his statement.

Baseball commissioner Ford Frick demanded to see Robinson. Robinson thought that surely the commissioner would explode in a rage, as everyone else had, over what had been said. Robinson was filled with trepidation, but when he sat down in Frick's office, he told the commissioner exactly what happened. Much to Robinson's surprise, Frick sat quietly and calmly. He asked for the details, then asked to be sent the transcript from the show. As the two men rose to shake hands, Frick said something that made a great impression on Robinson:

Jackie, I want you to know how I feel personally. Whenever you believe enough in something to sound off about it, whenever you feel strongly that you've got to come out swinging, I sincerely hope you'll swing the real heavy bat and not the fungo [a practice bat].[89]

Problems with Management

Jackie Robinson sometimes swung that "real heavy bat" against baseball management. In October 1950 Walter O'Malley replaced Branch Rickey as the Dodgers general manager and president. Not only was Robinson's mentor gone, but he was replaced by a man who didn't necessarily agree with the player's outspoken views. "I was not O'Malley's kind of black," Robinson said. "Campanella was." He made this comment after O'Malley indirectly criticized him for speaking out against the recent bombings of black churches in

Dodgers general manager Walter O'Malley (right) disagreed with Robinson's views on racism.

Miami, which were triggered by the Supreme Court's ruling that banned segregation in schools.[90]

Robinson challenged other authorities in professional baseball in addition to Dodgers management. In 1952, after being fined by National League president Warren Giles for yelling at an umpire, Robinson refused to play another game until he had a hearing with the president. Many in baseball were outraged by this behavior. They could not believe a player's flouting the authority of the league president. Dodgers general manager, Buzzy Bavasi, was astonished: "You can't tell the president of the league what to do."[91]

But Robinson was adamant. He believed that even a baseball player had a right to be heard in defense of himself, like all American citizens. He made this message clear to the league president and stayed away from the game until he had his hearing with Giles. Only then did he agree to return to the playing field.

Robinson Criticized

Cleveland star Larry Doby was critical of Robinson.

While Jackie Robinson strove to be a crusader for civil rights and fair treatment for all players, he was sometimes criticized for thinking too much of himself. Recalls Larry Doby, a one-time teammate of Robinson's and an All-Star who played with the Cleveland Indians for seventeen years:

Jackie had a large ego. . . . [He] appreciated and discussed his place in history and thought of himself in the same light as Paul Robeson and Joe Louis. He used to say baseball was the all-American game unless you were black, and that he was out to change that. It would be the all-American game for everybody.[92]

Robinson's ego and sensitive nature sometimes led to uncomfortable moments. A man of pride and with a strong sense of history, he sometimes overreacted to innocent matters, treating them as if they were racial attacks.

For instance, there was the watermelon incident outside Shibe Stadium in Philadelphia one sweltering summer afternoon in 1950. The Dodgers had just finished a game and were leaving the stadium. An old man with a tray full of watermelon

On Ebbets Field

In The Greatest Stories Ever Told About Baseball, *Kevin Nelson, the baseball writer, talks about Ebbets Field, home of the Brooklyn Dodgers, and what it meant to be a Brooklyn fan growing up in the forties and fifties:*

"To read accounts of post-war Brooklyn by writers sympathetic to the Dodgers is to go back to a simpler, greener world that has now been lost.

The television was not omnipresent. In the hot weather people sat around on the stoops gabbing with their neighbors. Kids played ball on the streets. There were no [drug] pushers and thugs around, people went out at night without fear.

The neighborhoods were still strong. Brooklyn was broken into distinct ethnic areas—Italians, Irish, the Jews—where the people watched out for their own and took care of them. The streets were clean and not clogged with cars. In the afternoons or evenings, you tuned in Red Barber to get the game. In the morning, you picked up the paper to see the box scores or get the results of other games.

At the center of this small, bubbling universe was Ebbets Field. The fans at Wrigley [Field, in Chicago] or Fenway [Park, in Boston] or any of the older downtown parks still standing can probably best appreciate what Ebbets meant to followers of the Dodgers. It was their home away from home—a green place, a safe spot. And it was, by all accounts, a wonderful place to watch a baseball game.

Red Barber said, 'When you have a box seat at Brooklyn, you are practially playing the infield.' According to one eyewitness, you were so close to the action on the field that you could see the cords in a player's neck tighten."

slices stood by the exit and offered the grateful players a free slice. Robinson was the last to exit, and when the man held the watermelon slice right up to his face, Robinson exploded. He ranted and raved, accusing the old man of bigotry. The man shrank back in horror. When Robinson finally stamped up the steps of the team bus, he saw that everyone else had a slice of watermelon in his hand.

There was also the time Pee Wee Reese was honored on his birthday at Ebbets Field. All the fans were given candles, which they lit when the stadium lights were turned out. In salute to the infielder from Kentucky, a Confederate flag was raised and a singer sang "Dixie." Carl Erskine remembered Robinson's reaction: "Well, I looked at Jackie's face, and his skin was pulled tight. He was as angry as I had ever seen him. He took that whole scene as a personal insult and let everybody know about it."[93]

Other ballplayers understood Robinson's difficult position as a black man in a white sport. "He was hot-tempered in my opinion," said teammate Carl Erskine, "only because he was martyred."[94] Robinson himself admitted to a bad temper. "I had too much stored up inside me," Robinson admitted. "I blamed it on the fact that I wasn't able to squawk when I thought I had a squawk coming."[95]

Newspapers could be harsh with Robinson about his temper. Popular columnist Red Smith asserted that Robinson was not

Robinson's troubles off the field did not affect his play on the field. He continued to play hard and well and to strive for excellence in all aspects of his game.

As a young player, Joe Black took Robinson's advice not to let racism affect his play.

But Wilson Woodbeck, public relations director of the National Association of Negro Musicians, was among those moved by Robinson's constant struggle and by his understanding of Robinson's flaring temper. "Jackie was a few years ahead of his time. It's always time to do what's right, but the power structure does not always see it that way. Jackie carried so many burdens, took so much abuse. So many times, he lost sight of himself for others."[98]

Performance Did Not Suffer

Controversy off the field did not hurt Robinson's performance on the field. Many white players were impressed by his determination to succeed. "Everybody knew the pressure Jackie was under from the incidents, the name-calling from the stands, the crazy letters he got, all that stuff," said teammate Spider Jorgenson. "There was no such thing as just have a good day or a bad day on the field. Everything was measured against history."[99]

Robinson's determination affected black ballplayers as well. Joe Black, like Robinson, endured the slurs, taunts, and threats from the stands on many occasions. Black would be boiling inside at the abuse, when Robinson would come up quietly behind him and put his hand on the younger man's shoulder and tell him to just play good baseball. "You can't fight. Maybe someday, but not now. You can't fight."[100]

Who knew this better than Jackie Robinson?

only racist but paranoid, too: "I thought he saw racism and prejudice under the bed and I'd get out of patience with things he'd say."[96] "You owe a great deal to the game," said the *Sporting News* in an open letter to Robinson in 1955, trying to shame him into being less outspoken. A few years earlier the same publication had admonished him for his unchecked words—this time for not being a good representative of his people: "There are definite restraints under which Jackie must place himself, and definite obligations which, as the first Negro in the modern history of the majors, he owes to his race."[97]

6 Final Years in Baseball

During the early fifties Robinson proved to be one of the best players in baseball. His hitting was as reliable as ever, and he could always be counted on for poking a line drive through the opposition to get runners home. As second baseman for the Dodgers, he did not fear contact with opposition runners. As a base runner himself, he was an exciting player to watch. During one game, Philadelphia pitcher Robin Roberts picked Robinson off first base. Robinson argued strenuously with the umpire for what he thought was a bad call. His next time up, Robinson made a base hit, raced to third base on a hit, and then stole home. "That made up for the bad call against him," mused Roberts.[101]

One of Robinson's greatest moments in baseball came on the final day of the 1951 season. The Dodgers needed to win this game against the Philadelphia Phillies in order to play the crosstown rival New York Giants for the National League pennant.

The Phillies and the Dodgers fought hard, and the game went into extra innings. In the bottom of the twelfth inning,

Jackie lunges to tag an opponent sliding into second base. His play seemed to improve as he got older.

tied his previous year's home run tally with nineteen, and his season batting average was an impressive .308. The Dodgers failed to win the World Series, though: in the seventh and deciding game for the pennant against the Yankees, Robinson, at bat in the seventh inning with the Dodgers behind, popped up, ending the Dodgers rally.

The following year the Dodgers won the pennant by thirteen games. Many Dodgers players had a terrific season, including Robinson, who hit .329 with ninety-five RBIs (runs batted in). But once again, the Dodgers failed to win the World Series against the Yankees. Robinson was

In his first game as shortstop, Robinson leaps to spear a line drive. In his career as a Dodger, he played every infield position.

Robinson's great speed allowed him to steal bases often. Here, he steals home against the Chicago Cubs.

with the Phillies threatening to score, Robinson made a miraculous diving catch, saving the Dodgers from certain elimination. At bat in the top of the fourteenth inning, Robinson dug his heels in and smashed a home run over the left field wall, ensuring a win and a place in the playoffs for the Dodgers. In the pennant race against the Giants, the Dodgers lost the third and deciding game when Bobby Thompson of the Giants hit his famous game-winning home run.

In 1952 Robinson led the Dodgers to the National League pennant, which they won by four-and-one-half games. Robinson

The Rundown

In The Boys of Summer *Roger Kahn recalls Robinson's thrilling exploits and the effect he had on frustrated opponents:*

"Once Russ Meyer, a short-tempered righthander, pitched a fine game against the Dodgers. The score going into the eighth inning was 2 to 2, and it was an achievement to check the Brooklyn hitters in Ebbets Field. Then, somehow, Robinson reached third base. He took a long lead, threatening to steal home, and the Phillies, using a set play, caught him fifteen feet off base. A rundown developed. This is the major league version of a game children call getting in a pickle. The runner is surrounded by fielders who throw the ball back and forth, gradually closing the gap. Since a ball travels four times faster than a man's best running speed, it is only a question of time before the gap closes and the runner is tagged. Except for Robinson. The rundown was his greatest play. Robinson could start so fast and stop so short that he could elude anyone in baseball, and he could feint [fake] a start and feint a stop as well.

All the Phillies rushed to the third-base line, a shortstop named Granny Hamner and a second baseman called Mike Goliat and the first baseman, Eddie Waitkus. The third baseman, Puddin' Head Jones, and the catcher Andy Seminick, were already there. Meyer himself joined. Among the gray uniforms Robinson in white lunged, and sprinted and leaped and stopped. The Phils threw the ball back and forth, but Robinson anticipated their throws, and after forty seconds, and six throws, the gap had not closed. Then, a throw toward third went wild and Robinson made his final victorious run at home plate. Meyer dropped to his knees and threw both arms around Robinson's stout legs. Robinson bounced a hip against Meyer's head and came home running backward, saying 'What the hell are you trying to do?'

'Under the stands, Robinson,' Meyer said.

'Right now,' Robinson roared.

Police beat them to the proposed ring. Robinson not only won games; he won and infuriated the losers."

moved to left field to make room for young Jim Gilliam at second base. In 1954 the Dodgers were beaten out of the pennant race by the Giants.

Robinson was thirty-five years old at the end of the 1954 season. Ballplayers thought about retirement well before that age. At thirty-five, a baseball player was considered to be an old man among the young rookies of eighteen and nineteen and the "seasoned veterans" just approaching their thirties. Beset by injuries, including bad knees and a sore shoulder, Robinson often felt like an old man that season. The vision of winning a World Series, once clear in his mind's eye, had begun to fade.

At Last, a World Series Win

In 1955 Jackie Robinson pushed himself to his limits to help his team achieve baseball's ultimate goal: victory in the World Series.

In the 1955 World Series Robinson and the Dodgers again faced the New York Yankees. The Dodgers knew they weren't as strong as the Yankees in many respects. For one thing, the Yankees had better hitters; for another, youth was clearly on their side. Consequently, the Dodgers weren't really fired up for competition. Early in the first game, standing on third base with two men out, Robinson decided to do

Robinson safely steals home against Yogi Berra and the Yankees in the first game of the 1955 World Series. Jackie's daring play inspired his lagging teammates.

something about it. As the Yankee pitcher went into his windup, Robinson suddenly broke for home plate. He sped down the base path—racing the pitched ball to home plate—and slid in under the tag of catcher Yogi Berra. "Safe!" cried the umpire. In the Dodgers dugout players leaped to their feet, cheering and clapping each other on the back. Although the Dodgers eventually lost that first game, their fire had been rekindled.

The Yankees won the second game, too, but the Dodgers took the next three back at Ebbets Field. The Yankees won the sixth game, and the final and deciding engagement was held at Ebbets Field. But Robinson did not play; suffering from pains in his legs, he had to remain on the bench.

With their finest pitcher, Johnny Podres, on the mound, the Dodgers jumped to an early lead and were able to maintain it until the very end. Roy Campanella, the

Bill Skowron trots to first base after blasting a three-run homer in the sixth game of the 1955 World Series. The Yankees won the game to tie the series and go to the seventh and deciding game against Jackie Robinson and the Dodgers.

No Blacks in Management

In his biography of Robinson, First of the Chosen Few, *Joseph Nazel writes about how Jackie Robinson would have liked to have accepted a job as the first black baseball manager in the major leagues— but the position was never offered. Nazel suggests an explanation:*

"Blacks were just not ready to take over the responsibilities of management, said the major league owners. What they meant was, there was no advantage to be gained by hiring a black manager. What if the players refused to play for him because he was black? It was too much to risk for the return.

Twenty years would pass—after Jackie Robinson's retirement from baseball—before the color-line barring blacks from management positions was seriously attacked. Even then it was only a token gesture, designed to take some of the pressure off baseball. . . . For a single season, 1975-1976, Frank Robinson, black baseballer . . . managed for the Cleveland Indians. The Indians weren't winning when Robinson took charge of the team and the season was a disappointing one. Upper management fired the manager, and black Americans cried out—'Last hired, first fired!' The old adage was not so old after all."

Dodgers catcher, later remembered the closing moments of that decisive game:

We were still leading 2-0 when Podres left the dugout for the final inning. The players on the bench, getting more nervous by the minute, began telling John how to pitch for the last three outs.

Leave him alone! I hollered. Don't everybody tell him how to pitch. He did all right by himself for eight innings.

Podres got three [out] in a row. Bill Skowron popped up. Bob Cerv struck out. Elston Howard—the last man that stood between the Dodgers and their first world championship in history—swung at a 2-2 pitch and sent a routine grounder to Reese who threw him out at first; and we finally beat the Yankees.[102]

Podres, the winning pitcher, recalled the excitement and jubilation in Brooklyn that night: "I never knew how important that was to the people of Brooklyn until I got back to my hotel that night and they were gathered out there, thousands of them to welcome me back. They carried on all night, and there was just no sleeping. It was wonderful."[103] Despite his lack of participation in the final game, Robinson would later recall that winning the World Series was "one of the greatest thrills of my life."[104]

Looking Toward the Future

Despite the Dodgers having won the World Series, Robinson was not content during the 1956 season. As in the previous season, his batting average was down and he was not playing all the time. His knees were bothering him. Rumors of his departure were spreading, and he was prepared for it. He was looking into his future.

Robinson focused outside of baseball for opportunities. During that difficult 1956 season he met with William Black of Chock Full O' Nuts, a company that produced coffee and owned a chain of small restaurants around the country, which were operated mostly by blacks. The executive wanted Robinson for an important management position in the company: he would work as public relations director. At the same time, *Look* magazine came to Robinson with a high-paying offer for an exclusive story about his retirement. The time seemed ripe to leave baseball.

But Jackie wanted to be fair to the Dodgers. Years later he recalled the delicate situation:

> I couldn't talk to anyone about my plans because negotiations with *Look* and Chock were not concluded. If the story leaked to the press, I would lose out on the *Look* story, and if the Chock negotiations broke down, I would face an insecure future with the Dodgers. It was touch and go.[105]

Robinson was determined to take care of his interests. Though contacted by the Dodgers executives with an urgent request

Robinson poses with his letter of resignation to the Giants, which is written on his new employer's stationery.

Newly retired from baseball, Jackie relaxes at home with his family. The walls are covered with the many trophies Robinson earned in his ten years as a major league player.

for a special meeting, he put them off for a day and signed his contract with Chock Full O' Nuts. The next day he went to the meeting with the Dodgers management and was informed that he had been traded to the New York Giants.

Robinson wanted to tell the Dodgers at that moment that he was not theirs anymore to be traded—that he had already signed a contract with Chock Full O' Nuts —but because of the *Look* offer, he said nothing. Robinson then went to the Giants

and asked them to keep quiet about the trade. They asked why, but Robinson couldn't tell them! He didn't want to ruin the *Look* offer.

The Giants went ahead and announced the trade to the press, and the Robinson house in Connecticut was immediately besieged by reporters. Robinson and his family kept their lips buttoned for days until *Look* hit the newsstands with the exclusive story. Unfortunately, some *Look* subscribers received their copies three days before the edition was available at newsstands, and the press found out about the story. *Look* executives urged Robinson to come into New York and talk to the press.

At this time the Giants offered Robinson $60,000 to reconsider his decision to quit baseball. It was a compelling offer, but after the Dodgers management suggested that Robinson was bargaining to get more money from the Giants, Robinson adamantly restated his decision. He was finished with baseball.

Some reporters criticized Robinson for having held out on the story. As Maury Allen reports:

The daily newspaper reporters were stung by the retirement announcement in *Look* magazine. They resented Robinson for "retiring" [exclusively] to a magazine and not with the ritualistic press conference before the beat reporters he had been associated with for so many years. Reporters were simply

In 1962, forty-one-year-old Jackie Robinson and his proud family celebrate the final triumph of his baseball career: his induction into the Hall of Fame.

jealous of the attention the *Look* article received. . . . They had been scooped badly on a big story by a magazine. It hurt. They answered back as they could. They offered slurs at Robinson's character. Some would exact vengeance for this slight for several years to come.[106]

Robinson said in *Look* that he would miss baseball:

But now I'll be able to spend more time with my family. My kids and I will get to know each other better. Jackie, Sharon and David will have a real father they can play with and talk to in the evening and every weekend. They won't have to look for him on TV.

Maybe my sons will want to play ball, as I have, when they grow up. I'd love it if they do. But I'll see to it they get a college education first, and meet the kind of people who can help them later.

Just now Jackie still feels badly about my quitting. It's tough for a ten-year-old to have his dad suddenly turn from a ballplayer to a commuter. I guess it will be quite a change for me, too. But someday Jackie will realize that the old man quit baseball just in time.[107]

A Final Salute from Baseball

Jackie Robinson had a distinguished career in baseball. In his ten seasons with the Brooklyn Dodgers—the only major league team he played for—the Dodgers won six National League pennants, in 1947, 1949, 1952, 1953, 1955, and 1956. His lifetime batting average was a very respectable .311. He hit a total of 137 home runs, with a high of 19 each in 1951 and 1952. He stole a total of 197 bases, and stole home plate on 11 occasions, including the most memorable, spirit-lifting steal in his first World Series game against the Yankees in 1955.

It was no surprise to any baseball fan when Robinson was inducted into the National Baseball Hall of Fame upon his first eligibility in 1962.

Chapter

7 On to Another Stage

By the time of his admission to the Baseball Hall of Fame in 1962, Jackie Robinson had distanced himself from the sport. In 1958, when Ebbets Field was razed to make room for a low-income housing development, Robinson was unsentimental. "I don't feel anything. They need these apartment buildings more than they need a monument to baseball. I've had my thrills."[108] Being admitted to the Hall of Fame pleased him, but he kept this honor in perspective: "If it meant I had to give up anything I did or said, the Hall of Fame would have to go its own way. I did what I thought was right and, to me, right is more important than any honor."[109]

Jackie Robinson had seen his career in major league baseball as merely a stage in his life, and he had gone on to what he considered more important things. He committed himself to other causes that worked toward the eradication of the color barrier. The tremendous ability he displayed on the field was exceeded only by his energy and commitment off the field. Making use of his baseball notoriety, Robinson continued his efforts to improve the lives of blacks.

While fulfilling his two-year contract as vice president of personnel at Chock Full O' Nuts, Robinson's job was to keep track of the one thousand employees (80 percent of whom were black), and keep turnover to a minimum. Rachel Robinson remembers her husband's experience:

> He loved that job. He wanted an active position and that job was certainly active. He had access to the employees, and he would visit several of the stores each day. He would get involved in their personal lives. He would talk to them about everything: about budgeting their salaries or saving their money or dealing with their kids. He talked to the women who were raising large families on their own, and he would talk to the men who had just gotten out of jail to their first job. He seemed to be everywhere with those people. He even started a company summer camp for the children of employees.[110]

Robinson obviously found satisfaction in this position, but something was missing. Somehow he had to reach more people.

While still employed by Chock Full O' Nuts, Robinson was asked by the *New York Post* to write three newspaper columns every week, dealing with any issues he chose. Sometimes he wrote about baseball, but he usually discussed politics and international affairs. The *Post* gave him free rein, and Robinson's thoughts and opinions—usually controversial—poured out into newsprint.

On April 28, 1959, in his first column, Robinson introduced himself to his readers and explained that he would be writing about the upcoming 1960 presidential campaign and other domestic issues, foreign affairs, and even baseball. He stated, too, that although he spoke for himself, as he had always done, he hoped to strike a sympathetic chord with black readers—"to touch on some things that many of us commonly share and feel."[111]

In response to columns expressing outrage and contempt for the treatment of blacks, mail flowed in to the *New York Post* and Chock Full O' Nuts. Some letters supported him, but most took issue with his opinions. At one point readers threatened to boycott the Chock Full O' Nuts restaurants because of Robinson's opinions. Despite the threat, Robinson was supported by the president of the company, William Black, who wrote him a letter of encouragement. Black told Robinson to keep speaking up, and that anyone who wanted to switch brands of coffee was welcome to do so!

The Freedom National Bank

From his experience at Chock Full O' Nuts, Robinson got a first-hand look at the way the American business structure worked. He realized that, for blacks to gain economic equality with whites, they had to know more about the way American business worked, and they had to become involved with it. In his autobiography Robinson explained:

I became fascinated with the way big business was conducted, with the operation of the stock market and the power which exists in the board rooms of banks and corporations. Black people were coming to the point where they would be crying out in behalf of Black Power, but it was pathetic to realize how little we knew of money. The financial establishment of America was as much a mystery to us as we were to the establishment. I recall that when I first joined Chock, after leaving baseball, my picture was used on the financial pages of the *New York Times,* and a very knowledgeable newsman told me that it was the first time a black man's picture had been featured in that section.[112]

The banking industry, dominated by whites, did not cater to the needs of blacks, and distrust was a key element of this failing: "By and large, in the banking business, blacks were considered bad credit risks,

Robinson began a new stage of his life in 1957 as vice president of personnel for the Chock Full O' Nuts Company. He poses here with company president William Black.

MR. JACK R. ROBINSON
VICE PRESIDENT

After Baseball, He Did Not Have to Keep His Mouth Shut

In Roger Kahn's nostalgic book, The Boys of Summer, *he remembers an incident with Jackie Robinson over lunch in Manhattan, when an elderly man stopped by their table for an autograph:*

"'Please,' said a short, elderly man, bending so that his bald head dropped between us. 'Be a good boy and give your autograph.'

'What?' Robinson's tenor clanged through the restaurant.

The man started. 'I said, could I have your autograph?'

'That isn't what you said.' Robinson's voice drew eyes toward our table. The man was frightened. 'Who's this for?' Robinson shouted.

'My grandson.'

'All right. I'll give you the autograph to your grandson, but not because I'm a boy.' Robinson scribbled on the menu. The man took it and hurried away.

'You're a fierce bastard,' I said.

'He won't call a black man "boy" again,' said Robinson."

not only because of their median low income compared to that of whites, but because of the stereotype which had existed for many years that they were not to be trusted. . . ." Because they were considered bad credit risks, blacks found it extremely difficult to get loans from banks to buy homes or start up their own businesses. Robinson himself had heard a friend speak of a white bank president in Connecticut who "had never known a Negro in whom he had confidence for more than a $300 loan."[113]

With the help of several skilled and experienced business partners, Robinson launched the Freedom National Bank in New York City in 1964, and years of success followed. The bank eased restrictions on lending money to poor people, and many residents took out loans unavailable at any other bank in the city. As Robinson explained in his autobiography, "With regard to certain internal affairs, there are some ways that we had to be different because we were a black bank. Without being loose in policies, we had to be a lot less rigid than white banks had been under similar circumstances."[114]

Moreover, Harlemites were delighted to have a bank that was black owned and where they knew their needs would be addressed without prejudice by the bank officers. The bank president, William Hudgins, even declared that anyone could come to him directly to discuss any problem. Proud Harlem residents passed the word about the bank to their friends and relatives, in Harlem and beyond. More and more individuals and institutions put their money into the bank. From its founding in 1964, it grew to become the largest of the black banks in the nation.

But success was not insured. The bank lost large amounts of money on bad loans for several years. Robinson grew concerned that it was in trouble. When examiners from the state comptroller's office performed routine checks of bank operations, they always told Robinson that things ran well at Freedom Bank. Only when it was almost too late did Robinson find out that they had lied to him because they did not want to be charged with racism for criticizing a black business! From then on the comptroller's office gave Robinson the truth—that there was serious financial trouble at Freedom Bank. The bank narrowly avoided failure and for more than twenty years successfully helped many homeowners and small business people in Harlem realize their material dreams. In November 1990, suffering from increased defaults on bad loans and other internal problems, Freedom National Bank was declared insolvent and was shut down by federal regulators.

Robinson and Nixon

Just as he saw business as a way to effect change, Robinson also thought politics would be a good vehicle. In 1960 he campaigned for Republican candidate Richard M. Nixon, who would face Democrat John F. Kennedy in that year's presidential election.

Before joining the Republican campaign, however, Robinson had approached Kennedy and grilled him about his stand

Robinson shakes hands with Republican presidential candidate Richard Nixon during the 1960 campaign. Jackie was eventually disappointed with Nixon's position on civil rights.

on the status of blacks in America and how that status should change. Robinson was not at all impressed with the young Massachusetts senator's response:

> John Kennedy said, 'Mr. Robinson, I don't know much about the problems of colored people since I come from New England.' I figured, the hell with that. Any man in Congress for fifteen years ought to make it his business to know colored people.[115]

Even though Robinson backed Nixon, it soon seemed that Nixon was not really backing Robinson. The Republican candidate did not agree with many of Robinson's recommendations. Robinson wanted Nixon to speak to the citizens of Harlem, and Nixon would not. Robinson insisted

Robinson decided not to support John F. Kennedy for president after Kennedy admitted knowing little about the problems of black people in America.

Robinson and Rockefeller

Despite his discouraging experience with Nixon in 1960, Robinson was not yet through with national politics. In 1964 he worked for New York governor Nelson Rockefeller in his run against Arizona senator Barry Goldwater for the Republican nomination for the upcoming presidential election. Robinson agreed to back Rockefeller only after the New York governor had made many changes in his administration in line with the suggestions of a group of local black leaders led by Robinson. Once again Robinson showed his color-blind loyalty to men he considered allies in the fight for civil rights. However, Goldwater was chosen by the Republican Party at the San Francisco convention in 1964.

Goldwater would face the Democratic nominee, incumbent President Lyndon B. Johnson, in the election, and Robinson was frightened. Goldwater was backed by conservative whites, Johnson by blacks

Robinson supported Nelson Rockefeller (left) for president in 1964. Rockefeller later lost the Republican nomination to Barry Goldwater.

that Nixon speak out against the controversial jailing of Martin Luther King Jr., in Georgia over a traffic violation, and Nixon did not. Nixon also insisted on being photographed with an arch-segregationist former justice of the Supreme Court. To Robinson, Nixon "had written off the Negro vote, and the Negroes responded by writing off Mr. Nixon."[116]

In 1968 Robinson's commitment to stick to his principles led him to campaign for Senator Hubert H. Humphrey against Nixon and his running mate, Spiro Agnew. He publicly condemned the Nixon-Agnew ticket as being racist. Robinson had to admit he had been wrong about Nixon. The man, he said, had done more harm than good for the country.

The Sixties

Robinson talks to reporters at the 1964 Republican National Convention in San Francisco. He accused Barry Goldwater, who eventually won the Republican candidacy, of bigotry.

The sixties were a turbulent time in American history. Many blacks had become increasingly radical. The message of black militants was heard in the media: It was one of separatism—pulling away politically and culturally from the white mainstream—and of pride. Blacks were supposed to embrace African values by adopting traditional hairstyles and clothing. According to one writer, blackness then was measured by "one's militancy, the race of a spouse, style of attire and darkness of skin."[120]

Robinson did not fit in with these kinds of changes. He did not feel it necessary to act in accordance with popular black opinion. His skin was definitely

and liberal whites, and Robinson feared this kind of election would divide the country. He had fought his greatest battles to bring people together and did not want to live in a country where political parties were segregated along the lines of color. "It would make everything I worked for meaningless."[117]

Robinson made his opinions of Goldwater clear in several newspaper columns and in interviews on national television and radio during the convention: "When I was asked my opinion of Barry Goldwater, I gave it. I said I thought he was a bigot."[118]

Goldwater was defeated by Johnson in the 1964 presidential election. Robinson was pleased by Johnson's victory and somewhat satisfied with what he himself had accomplished. "What with the columns I had written about Goldwater . . . and the television and radio interviews, I had achieved a great deal of publicity about the way I felt about Goldwater."[119]

Lyndon Baines Johnson defeated Barry Goldwater in the 1964 presidential election. Robinson was pleased with his own efforts to support LBJ's campaign.

black, and his militancy as the first black player in major-league baseball was unquestioned, but he also felt quite comfortable dressed in business suits and with his hair cut short. He was his own man. And because he wanted to change the system by working within it instead of against it, he had become an outsider. He found himself out of step. On speaking engagements at colleges, he was even booed and called an Uncle Tom for continuing to work with white society.

While it pained him that people seemed to forget what he had done for integration, Robinson learned to be philosophical about his diminishing status among blacks. He tried to understand the struggle between generations, as his wife Rachel would recall: "We had [the same struggle] with our own children. He listened and he learned from them. He changed in a lot of ways as he became more aware of their anger."[121]

Other Black Leaders

Robinson also worked with Martin Luther King Jr., whom he had met just before retiring from baseball. Throughout the sixties, he would offer his services to King wherever and whenever they were needed, including as fundraiser for rebuilding churches in Georgia that had been bombed and burned by antiblack citizens. Robinson, who had endured so much hatred, recognized and appreciated the qualities that made King a great leader: "Godliness, strength, courage, and patience in the face of overwhelming odds were his chief characteristics."[122]

Although he respected and admired King, Robinson never considered himself "a soldier in Martin's army." He freely admitted to his own inability to set aside his instinct for retaliation in the face of danger: "My reflexes aren't conditioned to

Dr. Martin Luther King Jr., speaks at a civil rights demonstration. Although Robinson admired King's leadership and character, he did not share King's belief in nonviolence.

Ideological rivals King and Malcolm X (right) share a rare moment of agreement at the nation's Capitol. Malcolm X thought Robinson was a "tool of the white bosses."

accept nonviolence in the face of violence-provoking attacks."[123]

Robinson continued to take unpopular stands, speaking out against those he thought were harmful to America, like Malcolm X. The Black Muslim leader and Robinson had many public differences. After defending United Nations undersecretary Ralph Bunche from an attack by Malcolm X, who had claimed that Bunche was being used by his white supervisors, Robinson too was verbally attacked by the Muslim leader. In Malcolm X's words, which were published in newspapers around the country, Robinson, like Bunche, was "a tool of white bosses . . . you let them use you to destroy Paul Robeson. You let your white boss send you before a congressional hearing in Washington, D.C. (the capital of Segregationville) to dispute

and condemn Paul Robeson, because he had these guilty American whites frightened silly."[124]

Robinson did not hesitate to defend himself. In his syndicated newspaper column Robinson declared, "I do nothing to please white bosses or black agitators, unless they are things that please me."[125] He also publicly repudiated Malcolm X's pleas for a separate black state in America, as well as various antiwhite statements. Robinson's proud and public declarations also exposed the militant black leader to criticism from some in the country's black leadership.

Privately, Robinson admired the black activist. He recognized Malcolm X as a proud, clean-living role model for black youth desperately in need of such a model. Upon learning of Malcolm X's assassination in 1965, Robinson was deeply moved. "A lot of blue went out of the sky and some warmth from the sun when the sinister news came," he said sadly.[126]

Final Years

Given his tremendous athletic ability and, later, his relentless output in various manners of protest, it always seemed as if Jackie Robinson had an inexhaustible store of energy. Late in his life, however, he had begun a battle with diabetes and had to take injections on a regular basis to keep it under control. He always kept private any discussion of his diabetes.

While he watched his own body deteriorate, Robinson also experienced the painful loss of friends and mentors. On December 9, 1965, Branch Rickey died. "The passing of Mr. Rickey," Robinson told the press, "is like losing a father. . . . Mr. Rickey's death is a great loss not only to baseball, but to America. His life was full, and I'm sure there are no regrets as far as fulfillment in life. I think he did it all."[127]

After Rickey died Robinson was stunned by the lack of response from other blacks in baseball. It was as if history had been forgotten.

> At Mr. Rickey's funeral . . . a couple of black players were there, and one of them said that although he had not known Mr. Rickey, he felt he owed him tribute because Mr. Rickey had

created the opportunity for him to play today. I could not understand why some of the other black superstars who earn so much money in the game today had not even sent flowers or telegrams.[128]

A few years passed, and death struck close to Robinson again. In 1968 Jackie was notified that his mother was ill. He grabbed the first plane to California, intent on helping his mother recover—but Mallie Robinson died before the plane reached the ground. Later that year he

---

Rickey's Death

When Branch Rickey died in 1965, few black athletes showed up at his funeral. Robinson was outraged. To him, it was as if black players were turning their backs on one of the men who had made it possible for them to compete in the major leagues. In Rickey and Robinson, *Harvey Frommer recalls Robinson's anger and Monte Irvin's explanation:*

"Branch Rickey died at 10:00 P.M. on December 9. It was just eleven days before his eighty-fourth birthday. . . . Strangely, few blacks attended the funeral of the man who had given Jackie Robinson the chance to break baseball's color line. Rickey had always refused to accept any public honors for signing Robinson. 'I have declined them all,' he said. 'To accept honors and public applause for signing a superlative ballplayer, I would be ashamed.'

Jackie Robinson was ashamed and angered at the skimpy black representation at the funeral. He criticized black athletes. 'Not even flowers or telegrams, and they're earning all that money,' he raged.

Monte Irvin felt 'the warm feeling for Branch Rickey had worn thin. Seemingly since Jackie had acted the way he did and became arrogant and alienated a lot of people, they might have associated Jack's arrogance with his association with Branch. They were grateful for what Branch had done, but the warm feeling wasn't there the way it was at the beginning.'"

himself would suffer a heart attack, then lose the sight in one eye and partial sight in the other eye.

In 1971 Robinson experienced another tragic loss: Jackie Robinson Jr., died in an automobile accident. He was found in his yellow MG sports car on the shoulder of the Merritt Parkway in Connecticut; he had been on his way to the family home in Connecticut. The coroner determined that death came from a broken neck. While their son's death came as a blow to the Robinsons, it was not entirely unexpected.

Always standing in his father's shadow, burdened with his father's name and the greatness he had achieved, Jackie Robinson Jr., had had a difficult life. He had been arrested in 1968 in Stamford, Connecticut, for possession of an illegal handgun and small amounts of marijuana and heroin. He had been in jail and had suffered from drug addiction. While young Jackie's parents did their best to advise and protect him, it seemed he had been bent on destroying his life with the same passion that his father had tried to build his own.

A few years before, Robinson had painfully outlined his son's life in an interview:

"He quit high school. He joined the Army. He fought in Vietnam and he was wounded. We lost him somewhere. I've had more effect on other people's kids than on my own.

"How do you feel about that, sir?" asked one reporter.

The gray-haired black man, Jackie Robinson, shook his head. "I couldn't have had an important effect on anybody's child if this happened to my own."[129]

In 1972, the year following his son's death, Jackie Robinson died. During that year he was often philosophical about his life, about his effect on baseball, about the son that he had lost. Sometimes he questioned his position among the country's black leadership, reflecting on the way times had changed while he had remained the same: "The baseball years seem very long ago. When I quit, I went into the NAACP, and the conservatives found me hard to take. They were men of eighty. Their attitude was: don't rock the boat. Today's militants find me hard to take. Their attitude is: burn everything. But I haven't changed much. . . ."[130]

No, he had not changed much at all— if changing meant becoming someone other than the man who had suffered terribly and succeeded grandly in the attempt to break down the color barrier in baseball. He was still the same Jackie Robinson.

The Country Has Lost a Great Man

Until the very end of his life, Jackie Robinson kept fighting for causes he believed in. He died of heart disease in Stamford, Connecticut, on the morning of October 24, 1972, at age fifty-three. He had been scheduled to attend a national drug symposium the day before, sponsored by the business community of Washington, D.C.

The funeral was held at Riverside Church in New York City. Jesse Jackson gave the eulogy, and the pallbearers were baseball players Ralph Branca, Larry Doby, Junior Gilliam, Don Newcombe, Pee Wee Reese, and basketball's Bill Russell. Thousands of tearful fans lined the streets as the coffin was carried to Cypress Hills Cemetery, where Jackie Robinson was laid to rest.

Personalities from the world of sports tried to find the right words to express their gratitude for Jackie Robinson. "If it hadn't been for Jackie," said basketball great Bill Russell, "I might never have become a professional basketball player."[131]

Elston Howard, the first black ballplayer on the New York Yankees, was, like many others, a friend of Robinson's. He wondered if young ballplayers understood the enormous struggle Robinson went through. "I don't think the young players would go through what he did. He did it

for all of us, for Willie Mays, Henry Aaron, Maury Wills, myself."[132]

Many important figures from the world of politics, including President Nixon and New York governor Nelson Rockefeller, expressed admiration for Robinson. Rockefeller remembered the man who campaigned for him:

Pallbearers carry Jackie Robinson's casket after his funeral services in 1972. Boston Celtics legend Bill Russell (first pallbearer on left) and many other celebrities took part in the ceremony.

The country has lost a great man, and I have lost a dear friend. Jackie Robinson and the Dodgers brought something uniquely American to Brooklyn, to New York, to America—competition, excitement, drama, laughter, tears, and above all, a lesson in how free peoples can and must learn to live together. Jackie Robinson proved how much one individual of [unconquerable] spirit can help to change a whole society.[133]

Robinson was praised by those active in civil rights as well, including Roy Innis, the national director of the Congress of Racial Equality: "A giant, a hero, and a great black man is lost forever. His life can never be recovered; we can only hope that his brilliant spirit serves as a guiding light

Rev. Jesse Jackson (right) comforts Robinson's wife, Rachel, and son David at Jackie's funeral.

for the generations of young black men following in his footsteps."[134]

Former teammates, too, had much to say about the man they had come to know well. Dixie Walker, Robinson's old opponent from their early days on the Dodgers, commented on his own change of heart: "I'm sad as could possibly be about his death. Me being a Southerner and raised in the South, it wasn't easy for me to accept Jackie when he came up. At that time I was resentful of Jackie and I made no bones about it. But he and I were shaking hands at the end."[135]

The Importance of Jackie Robinson

The game of baseball was the perfect place to watch integration work. In baseball blacks and whites shared the same playing field, worked together against an opposing team, consoled one another after mistakes were made, cheered for one another after fine plays. People across the country came to understand that merit came from excellence, not pigmentation.

Jackie Robinson was chosen to be the first black man to exhibit that excellence. He was in the right place at the right time—and he was certainly the right man for the job. A man with less intelligence, self-control, pride, commitment to civil rights, competitiveness, and athletic ability might surely have caused Branch Rickey's great experiment to fail. While such a failure would not have prevented integration, it surely would have made the process move at a slower pace. James ("Cool Papa") Bell, a contemporary of Robinson's in the Negro leagues, argued that Branch

Not Enough Understanding of the Past

Larry Doby was one of the greatest black players in the major leagues. He later became the first black manager in baseball and eventually worked in professional basketball as well. In Maury Allen's biography of Robinson, A Life Remembered, *Doby describes how he saw the rise in status of the black professional athlete, but questions whether something was missing from the success story:*

"I think of all that now, and I think there isn't enough understanding of the past. Not only by the fans and the press, also by the players. A guy like Dave Winfield makes twenty million dollars, and he can buy a house anywhere he wants and do anything he wants, but I don't think people understand why Winfield has this opportunity, what went before, just how hard things really were. I don't think kids are conscious of the past. . . . There is still a long way to go. Black players have to be better than white players. Black managers have to be better than white managers. . . . Young blacks don't know the history. . . . All they see is Winfield and the big money, and they want that. They are not interested in how anybody got here, what the conditions were, how hard we had to fight, how much abuse we had to take."

Larry Doby became the first black manager in major league baseball.

Rickey's choice of Robinson to break baseball's color barrier was a good one:

> We had a good level of ball, a lotta good players. We even had lights before the big leagues did. . . . As far as Jackie Robinson was concerned he was good enough to play in our all-star game in 1945, I remember that. He played shortstop for the West team. He was an outstanding runner. As far as being the one to break the color line, maybe there were some better players but as things turned out he was the right man for the job. Maybe they weren't looking for the best player, they were looking for an intelligent young man who could handle what had to be handled. He certainly proved he could do it, didn't he?[136]

He certainly did. With Robinson's success, the integration of baseball was under way, and color barriers began to crumble in cities and towns around the country. Years before the sixties and the boycotts, protest marches, and sit-ins for racial equality, black athletes—from baseball first, then from other sports—had already broken down many color barriers by sitting in all-white restaurants or sleeping in all-white hotels.

Expressing a Deep Outrage

Jackie Robinson's newspaper column in the New York Post *became a forum for black protest. Regarding the lynching of Mack Charles Parker in Mississippi, Robinson poured out his anger in his column:*

"Well, they said it couldn't happen any more. We're making tremendous progress, they said, so go slow on 'forcing' the issue. Go slow on civil rights legislation, school integration and law enforcement against violence by Southern bigots.

Yet last Friday night a quiet, hooded, well-drilled group of men entered an unguarded jailhouse in Mississippi. And when they left they took with them a screaming, beaten, bloodied human being.

It has happened here in our own America, and in 1959.

I can't really express my deep outrage about this terrible incident. I can only point out that the handwriting has been on the wall for all to see for quite a while. The lynching of Mack Parker is but the end result of all the shouts of defiance by Southern legislatures, all the open incitement to disobey the law by Southern governors, and all the weak-kneed gradualism of those entrusted with enforcing and protecting civil rights."

Jackie Robinson walks in a civil rights picket line during the 1960s. Robinson successfully mixed sports and politics.

Not Just Another Ballplayer

From the time of his momentous meeting with Branch Rickey, Robinson had known he could never be just another ballplayer. He would constantly be in the public eye, and every bat of an eyelash or disapproving frown from him would be translated by the media into some important statement on race relations. He did not have the luxury of simply playing good baseball.

It was clear to him that he needed to stand up to hatred and prejudice with dignity. In order to succeed, he had to show he could turn the other cheek to intolerance and injustice, and that he could play well, too. And he did both.

Consequently, Jackie Robinson became a hero and a symbol of pride and hope for black Americans everywhere. Throughout the country, in great cities and small towns, blacks who had never swung a bat nor felt the smoothness of a cowhide mitt on their hands suddenly became baseball fans! They packed the stadiums to see a fellow black compete against whites in a white man's game. They were proud of what they saw, too. Robinson's competitive spirit, his daring base running, game-saving defensive gems, and game-winning blasts off the powerful swing of his bat—all served to lift the spirits of black Americans and show them the potential for greatness within them all.

Jackie Robinson had a great influence on white Americans, too. Wearing a baseball uniform, he was like any man seeking justice and a fair shake—and any white man could sympathize with that. He was not demanding black power, and, as a result, whites found him nonthreatening. They heard his proud, intelligent voice on the radio or read his sophisticated comments in the newspapers, and they learned that blacks were worthy of respect and fair treatment. They accepted him.

On a personal level, Jackie's many friendships and his unending efforts at informing and advising young blacks in baseball touched many individuals, as did his involvement after baseball with civil rights organizations.

Jackie Robinson was more than just a great baseball player. Before baseball he had challenged segregation in the military. During his career with the Royals and the Dodgers, he broke down color barriers in cities and towns across the nation. After his superlative ten years with the Dodgers, he continued to work tirelessly in the

Robinson Acknowledges Rickey

In an article in the New York Times Robinson looks back on his time with Branch Rickey:

"I think the Rickey Experiment, as I call it, the original idea, would not have come about as successfully with anybody other than Mr. Rickey. The most important results of it are that it produced understanding among whites and it gave black people the idea that if I could do it, they could do it, too, that blackness wasn't subservient to anything."

struggle for civil rights. He devoted his life to fighting racial discrimination.

Mack Robinson sums up the importance of his brother's breaking of baseball's color barrier:

> From time to time, I'm watching sporting events, and I look at the TV screen, and I see Jackie Robinson. I look at the whole spectrum of black America's life from 1947 on [compared to] 1900 to 1947. We're no longer the servants, the butlers, the maids. We're senators, congressmen, mayors. We are baseball managers. I trace it back to Jack's breaking the color line and creating a social revolution in a white man's world. Blacks have excelled in all areas because Jack and Branch Rickey showed the world we could.[137]

They certainly did show the world. But it was Robinson, alone in the spotlight, who had to prove himself every day in the media or on the playing field. Perhaps his greatest attribute on the field was his competitiveness—something not measured in the box scores, but invaluable to the success of a sports team. In an interview after he retired from baseball, Robinson recalled his influence on an opposing team:

> I think the most symbolic part of Jackie Robinson, ballplayer, was making the pitcher believe he was going to the next base. I think he enjoyed that the most, too. I think my value to the Dodgers was disruption—making the pitcher concentrate on me instead of on my teammate, who was at bat at the time.[138]

In his glorious life, Jackie Robinson made a lot of disruptions—both on the field and off.

Notes

Introduction: Something to Remember

1. Maury Allen, *Jackie Robinson: A Life Remembered*. New York: Franklin Watts, 1987.

Chapter 1: Early Life

2. W. Sherman Savage, *Blacks in the West*. Westport, Connecticut: Greenwood Press, 1976.

3. Maury Allen, *Jackie Robinson*.

4. Maury Allen, *Jackie Robinson*.

5. Jackie Robinson, *I Never Had It Made*. New York: G. P. Putnam's Sons, 1972.

6. Jackie Robinson, *I Never Had It Made*.

7. Maury Allen, *Jackie Robinson*.

8. Jackie Robinson, *I Never Had It Made*.

9. Jackie Robinson, *I Never Had It Made*.

10. Maury Allen, *Jackie Robinson*.

11. Peter Golenbock, *Bums: An Oral History of the Brooklyn Dodgers*. New York: G. P. Putnam's Sons, 1984.

12. Maury Allen, *Jackie Robinson*.

13. Maury Allen, *Jackie Robinson*.

14. Leslie H. Fishel Jr. and Benjamin Quarels, *The Black American: A Documentary History*. New York: William Morrow and Company, 1970.

15. Jackie Robinson, *I Never Had It Made*.

16. Jackie Robinson, *I Never Had It Made*.

17. Jackie Robinson, *I Never Had It Made*.

18. Jackie Robinson, *I Never Had It Made*.

19. Jackie Robinson, *I Never Had It Made*.

20. Roger Kahn, *The Boys of Summer*. New York: Harper and Row, 1971.

21. Roger Kahn, *The Boys of Summer*.

Chapter 2: Rickey and Robinson

22. Art Rust Jr., *"Get That Nigger Off the Field!"*. New York: Delacorte Press, 1976.

23. Art Rust Jr., *"Get That Nigger Off the Field!"*

24. Art Rust Jr., *"Get That Nigger Off the Field!"*

25. Art Rust Jr., *"Get That Nigger Off the Field!"*

26. Art Rust Jr., *"Get That Nigger Off the Field!"*

27. Art Rust Jr., *"Get That Nigger Off the Field!"*

28. Art Rust Jr., *"Get That Nigger Off the Field!"*

29. Jules Tygiel, *Baseball's Great Experiment: Jackie Robinson and His Legacy*. New York: Oxford University Press, 1983.

30. Jules Tygiel, *Baseball's Great Experiment*.

31. Jules Tygiel, *Baseball's Great Experiment*.

32. Jeffrey Hart, *When the Going Was Good! American Life in the Fifties*. New York: Crown Publishers, 1982.

33. Harvey Frommer, *Rickey and Robinson: The Men Who Broke Baseball's Color Barrier*. New York: Macmillan Publishing, 1982.

34. Harvey Frommer, *Rickey and Robinson*.

35. Maury Allen, *Jackie Robinson*.

36. Maury Allen, *Jackie Robinson*.

37. Jules Tygiel, *Baseball's Great Experiment*.

38. Maury Allen, *Jackie Robinson*.

39. Harvey Frommer, *Rickey and Robinson*.

40. Jackie Robinson, *I Never Had It Made*.

41. Jules Tygiel, *Baseball's Great Experiment*.

42. Jackie Robinson, *I Never Had It Made.*

43. *New York Times,* October 25, 1972.

44. Jules Tygiel, *Baseball's Great Experiment.*

45. Jules Tygiel, *Baseball's Great Experiment.*

Chapter 3: A Difficult Strategy

46. Lerone Bennett Jr., *The Shaping of Black America.* Chicago: Johnson Publishing, 1975.

47. Neil A. Wynn, *The Afro-American and the Second World War.* New York: Holmes and Meier Publishers, 1976.

48. Jackie Robinson, *I Never Had It Made.*

49. Maury Allen, *Jackie Robinson.*

50. Jackie Robinson, *I Never Had It Made.*

51. Jackie Robinson, *I Never Had It Made.*

52. George R. Metcalf, *Black Profiles.* New York: McGraw-Hill Book Company, 1970.

53. Jackie Robinson, *I Never Had It Made.*

54. *New York Times,* October 25, 1972.

55. Maury Allen, *Jackie Robinson.*

56. Maury Allen, *Jackie Robinson.*

57. Jackie Robinson, *I Never Had It Made.*

58. Jackie Robinson, *I Never Had It Made.*

59. Jackie Robinson, *I Never Had It Made.*

60. Maury Allen, *Jackie Robinson.*

61. Joseph Nazel, *Jackie Robinson: First of the Chosen Few.* Los Angeles: Holloway House Publishing Company, 1982.

62. Maury Allen, *Jackie Robinson.*

63. Roger Kahn, *The Boys of Summer.*

64. Jackie Robinson, *I Never Had It Made.*

65. Jackie Robinson, *I Never Had It Made.*

66. Langston Hughes, Milton Meltzer, and Eric C. Lincoln, eds., *A Pictorial History of Black Americans.* 5th rev. ed. New York: Crown Publishers, 1983.

Chapter 4: Robinson Unleashed

67. Leslie H. Fishel Jr., and Benjamin Quarles. *The Black American.*

68. Harvey Frommer, *Rickey and Robinson.*

69. Jackie Robinson, *I Never Had It Made.*

70. Maury Allen, *Jackie Robinson.*

71. Jackie Robinson, *I Never Had It Made.*

72. Jules Tygiel, *Baseball's Great Experiment.*

73. Jules Tygiel, *Baseball's Great Experiment.*

74. Jules Tygiel, *Baseball's Great Experiment.*

75. Harvey Frommer, *Rickey and Robinson.*

76. Jackie Robinson, *I Never Had It Made.*

77. Jackie Robinson, *I Never Had It Made.*

78. Jackie Robinson, *I Never Had It Made.*

79. Martin Duberman, *Paul Robeson: A Biography.* New York: Ballantine Books, 1989.

80. Jackie Robinson, *I Never Had It Made.*

81. Jackie Robinson, *I Never Had It Made.*

82. Bosley Crowther, "The Jackie Robinson Story," *New York Times,* May 17, 1950.

Chapter 5: A Tireless Crusader

83. Jeffrey Hart, *When the Going Was Good!*

84. Jules Tygiel, *Baseball's Great Experiment.*

85. Jules Tygiel, *Baseball's Great Experiment.*

86. Jules Tygiel, *Baseball's Great Experiment.*

87. Jules Tygiel, *Baseball's Great Experiment.*

88. Jackie Robinson, *I Never Had It Made.*

89. George R. Metcalf, *Black Profiles.*

90. Harvey Frommer, *Jackie Robinson.* New York: Franklin Watts, 1984.

91. Jules Tygiel, *Baseball's Great Experiment.*

92. Maury Allen, *Jackie Robinson.*

93. Maury Allen, *Jackie Robinson.*

94. Jules Tygiel, *Baseball's Great Experiment.*

95. Jules Tygiel, *Baseball's Great Experiment.*

96. Jules Tygiel, *Baseball's Great Experiment.*

97. Jules Tygiel, *Baseball's Great Experiment.*

98. *New York Times,* October 28, 1972.

99. Maury Allen, *Jackie Robinson.*

100. Maury Allen, *Jackie Robinson.*

Chapter 6: Final Years in Baseball

101. Maury Allen, *Jackie Robinson.*

102. Roy Campanella, *It's Good to Be Alive.* Boston: Little, Brown, 1959.

103. Maury Allen, *Jackie Robinson.*

104. Jackie Robinson, *I Never Had It Made.*

105. Jackie Robinson, *I Never Had It Made.*

106. Maury Allen, *Jackie Robinson.*

107. Roger Kahn, *The Boys of Summer.*

Chapter 7: On to Another Stage

108. *New York Times,* October 25, 1972.

109. George R. Metcalf, *Black Profiles.*

110. Maury Allen, *Jackie Robinson.*

111. Maury Allen, *Jackie Robinson.*

112. Jackie Robinson, *I Never Had It Made.*

113. Jackie Robinson, *I Never Had It Made.*

114. Jackie Robinson, *I Never Had It Made.*

115. Roger Kahn, *The Boys of Summer.*

116. George R. Metcalf, *Black Profiles.*

117. Roger Kahn, *The Boys of Summer.*

118. Jackie Robinson, *I Never Had It Made.*

119. Jackie Robinson, *I Never Had It Made.*

120. Lena Williams, "In a 90s Quest for Black Identity, Intense Doubts and Disagreement," *New York Times,* November 30, 1991.

121. Maury Allen, *Jackie Robinson.*

122. Jackie Robinson, *I Never Had It Made.*

123. Jackie Robinson, *I Never Had It Made.*

124. Jackie Robinson, *I Never Had It Made.*

125. Harvey Frommer, *Jackie Robinson.*

126. Jackie Robinson, *I Never Had It Made.*

127. Harvey Frommer, *Jackie Robinson.*

128. Jackie Robinson, *I Never Had It Made.*

129. Roger Kahn, *The Boys of Summer.*

130. Roger Kahn, *The Boys of Summer.*

Epilogue: The Country Has Lost a Great Man

131. *New York Times,* October 25, 1972.

132. *New York Times,* October 25, 1972.

133. *New York Times,* October 25, 1972.

134. *New York Times,* October 25, 1972.

135. *New York Times,* October 25, 1972.

136. Maury Allen, *Jackie Robinson.*

137. Harvey Frommer, *Jackie Robinson.*

138. *New York Times,* October 25, 1972.

For Further Reading

Harvey Frommer, *Jackie Robinson*. New York: Franklin Watts, 1984.

Harvey Frommer, *Rickey and Robinson: The Men Who Broke Baseball's Color Barrier*. New York: Macmillan Publishing, 1982.

Joseph Nazel, *Jackie Robinson: First of the Chosen Few*. Los Angeles: Holloway House Publishing Company, 1982.

Kevin Nelson, *The Greatest Stories Ever Told About Baseball*. New York: Putnam Publishing Company, 1986.

Works Consulted

Maury Allen, *Jackie Robinson: A Life Remembered*. New York: Franklin Watts, 1987.

Lerone Bennett Jr., *Before the Mayflower: A History of Black America*. 5th ed. New York: Penguin Books, 1987.

Lerone Bennett Jr., *The Shaping of Black America*. Chicago: Johnson Publishing, 1975.

Roy Campanella, *It's Good to Be Alive*. Boston: Little, Brown, 1959.

Martin Duberman, *Paul Robeson: A Biography*. New York: Ballantine Books, 1989.

Leslie H. Fishel Jr. and Benjamin Quarles, *The Black American: A Documentary History*. New York: William Morrow and Company, 1970.

Peter Golenbock, *Bums: An Oral History of the Brooklyn Dodgers*. New York: G. P. Putnam's Sons, 1984.

Jeffrey Hart, *When the Going Was Good! American Life in the Fifties*. New York: Crown Publishers, 1982.

Langston Hughes, Milton Meltzer, and Eric C. Lincoln, eds., *A Pictorial History of Black Americans*. 5th rev. ed. New York: Crown Publishers, 1983.

Roger Kahn, *The Boys of Summer*. New York: Harper and Row, 1971.

Richard Lapchick, *Broken Promises: Racism in American Sports*. New York: St. Martin's Press, 1984.

George R. Metcalf, *Black Profiles*. New York: McGraw-Hill Book Company, 1970.

Mary Motley, ed., *The Invisible Soldier: The Experience of the Black Soldier, World War II*. Detroit: Wayne State University Press, 1975.

Jackie Robinson, *I Never Had It Made*. New York: G. P. Putnam's Sons, 1972.

Donn Rogosin, *Invisible Men: Life in Baseball's Negro Leagues*. New York: Athenum, 1983.

Art Rust Jr., *"Get That Nigger Off the Field!"*. New York: Delacorte Press, 1976.

W. Sherman Savage, *Blacks in the West*. Westport, CT: Greenwood Press, 1976.

Duke Snider, *The Duke of Flatbush*. New York: Zebra Books, 1988.

Jules Tygiel, *Baseball's Great Experiment: Jackie Robinson and His Legacy*. New York: Oxford University Press, 1983.

Neil A. Wynn, *The Afro-American and the Second World War*. New York: Holmes and Meier Publishers, 1976.

Index

Picture Credits

Cover photo by Culver Pictures, Inc.

AP/Wide World Photos, 7, 14(both), 19(top), 26, 27(bottom), 28(top), 43, 46, 47, 51, 52, 55(bottom), 58(both), 65, 66, 67, 79, 83, 90(bottom), 92, 93, 96, 97, 100

The Bettmann Archive, 34, 41

Library of Congress, 15, 90(top), 91(bottom)

National Archives, 16, 17, 38, 42, 62, 63, 87

National Baseball Library, Cooperstown, NY, 11, 24, 25(both), 29, 31(both), 32, 33, 35, 39, 49, 54, 69, 71(both), 72, 74, 75, 76, 84, 89

UPI/Bettmann, 8, 9, 12, 18, 19(bottom), 21, 27(top), 28(bottom), 40, 44, 45, 50, 53, 55(top), 56, 59, 60, 61, 64, 68, 77(both), 80, 82, 91(top), 98

About the Author

Arthur Diamond, born in Queens, New York, received a bachelor's degree in English from the University of Oregon and a master's degree in English/Writing from Queens College in New York.

Mr. Diamond is the author of several nonfiction books, including *The Bhopal Chemical Leak* and *Smallpox and the American Indian* in Lucent Books' World Disasters series. A writer and teacher, he lives in his boyhood home with his wife Irina and their children, Benjamin Thomas and Jessica Ann.